Read what church
about *Bullseye*...

"This ground-breaking project, *Bullseye*, is a challenge everyone needs to take"
—Pastor Jack Hayford, Founder and Chancellor, The King's University / Founder, The Church on the Way

"I highly recommend this important book so we speak clearly, boldly, and tenderly. Get it today!"
—Mike Bickle, Founder, International House of Prayer / Author & Prophetic Leader

"Take the Bullseye Challenge and learn God's perspective on the tough issues of today."
—RT Kendall, Former 25-year Minister of Westminster Chapel, London, Author of over 60 books

"The cry of my heart is that we think biblically and speak clearly. I highly recommend *Bullseye*"
—Bill Johnson, Bethel Church (Redding, California) / Author of *When Heaven Invades Earth*

"Here is the solution—our path to restoration and healing in America. Seize the opportunity"
—Dr. Michael Brown, President, FIRE School of Ministry / Author & Host of The Line of Fire radio program

"I join leaders across America and strongly encourage all to take the *Bullseye* Challenge!"
—Michael W. Smith, Internationally known Award-winning Singer/Songwriter

"This initiative is for world-changers! It tackles the issues and propels us to change lives."
—**Dr. Ché Ahn, Founding Pastor, HROCK Church (Pasadena, California) / President, Harvest International Ministry International / Chancellor, Wagner Leadership Institute**

"'Bullseye' usually refers to Satan's targeting of leaders. This is God redeeming the term for His glory"
—**James W. Goll, Founder of Encounters Network and Prayer Storm / International Best-Selling Author**

"I am so enthusiastic about the *Bullseye* Challenge! It's essential so we are equipped and empowered."
—**Dr. George Grant, Pastor, Professor, and Author**

"Here's God's gift to bring America back from destruction to our greatest awakening in history."
—**Bob Weiner, Weiner International Ministries / Founder, Maranatha Church and Campus Ministries / Author & Apostolic Leader**

"This book hits the *Bullseye* for the church today. If every Christian took this challenge, we could turn America around rapidly!"
—**Jennifer LeClaire, Senior Editor, *Charisma* Magazine / Director, Awakening House of Prayer / Author of *The Next Great Move of God***

"Ministering to youth across America, this is the tool we have been praying and waiting for."
—**Joe Oden, Assembly of God Evangelist / Author & Executive Director of Launch School of Evangelism**

"*Bullseye* empowers us to pull the bow and hit the target: righteousness in America. Do it!"
—**Lyndon Allen, Author / Radio Host of *Total Life Victory* Program / Leader with Christians United for Israel**

Bullseye

Congratulations! You are about to begin this exciting initiative to change your life. For the next 30 days, you will invest 15 minutes each day so you will "hit the mark"—understanding and communicating truth to our topsy-turvy world. Go to www.bullseyechallenge.com to watch the videos corresponding to the chapters. Together, we will make a difference for Jesus Christ.

Trade Paperback ISBN: 978-1-939447-96-8

Ebook ISBN: 978-1-939447-97-5

Library of Congress Control Number: 2016932831

Printed in the United States of America

Cover design by Jason Tomczak

**Unless otherwise noted, all scripture references
from King James Version of the Bible.**

Bullseye

Becoming Informed Influencers
in a Changing Culture

Larry Tomczak

Table of Contents

A Secular Worldview vs. a Spiritual Worldview

Preface
Twelve Influential Influencers

While writing this book over the span of two months, 265,000 (primarily young) people attended three music events in my Nashville "neighborhood." Two hundred thousand were at Bonnaroo and the CMA Music Festival, while 65,000 filled LP Field for the ageless Rolling Stones. What counters the "values" transmitted at these mega-events? Who's standing on point to reach the generations being so heavily influenced by today's pop culture?

The following twelve people, whom I've personally known as friends (most for 40 years or more), have helped lead the way. They've impacted my life by their authenticity and dedication to shape informed influencers in these turbulent times. There are many others, but these incredible servants are worthy of honor to the glory of God:

Che Ahn	Ron Luce
Frances Anfuso	Winkey Pratney
Mike Bickle	Chris Rogers
Mike Brown	Mat Staver
Chuck Colson*	Steve Strang
Lou Engle	Bob Weiner

Take the 30-day *Bullseye Challenge* and you'll communicate confidently on today's controversial issues. That's my promise to you!

—Larry Tomczak

---

*Chuck Colson mentored me through his writings and encouraged me significantly, but he has since passed from this life, leaving a legacy worth emulating.

Introduction

"One bullet to the back of my head and I'm done."

Standing in an inner-city alleyway as a college senior, those words flashed in my head. Picked up hitchhiking by some Cleveland thugs, it appeared that my life would be over in an instant. Yet God miraculously spared me to serve Him, and His people, for forty-five years.

I want my life to count. I believe that you do too. That's why you're holding this book and are about to embark on a journey to make yourself an informed influencer in today's rapidly changing culture. By investing 15 minutes daily for 30 days, your life will be changed as you apply yourself faithfully.

If you're a parent, this tool will train your family.

If you're a pastor, this is your secret weapon.

I pastored and planted churches for decades, so I know it's hard work. Barna Research revealed in 2015 that although ninety percent of Christian leaders believed that the Bible addresses most of today's controversial issues, only ten percent were bold enough to address them lest they lose people and tithes. If that's you, here's your resource to supply your adults and youth with what they need if you've been holding back.

So let's begin our journey. Let's enter the conversation. May the experience give you motivation, stimulation, and reflection 'til you cross the finish line!

Unity

"Every kingdom divided against itself will be ruined, and every
city or household divided against itself will not stand."
—Jesus Christ (Matt. 12:25)

Community

"To go fast, go alone. To go far, go together."
—African Proverb

Authenticity

"Our lives begin to end the day we become
silent about things that matter."
—Dr. Martin Luther King Jr.

Opportunity

"The optimist sees opportunity in every calamity.
A pessimist, calamity in every opportunity."
—Winston Churchill

Simplicity

"Make everything as simple as possible, but no simpler."
—Albert Einstein

Chapter 1
Apocalypse?

Is America on the brink of apocalyptic judgment? The stillness of the morning calm was about to be shattered by a series of explosions that would alter the course of human history. The time: 7:50 a.m. The date: Sunday, December 7, 1941. The place: Pearl Harbor.

Within a short time, bombers damaged eight battleships, destroying three—including the USS Arizona, which sank with 1,102 sailors on board. The Hickam and Wheeler air bases lost 177 planes. More than 2,400 servicemen and women lost their lives. The infamous, surprise attack would launch an entire nation into World War II.

But was this disaster really a surprise?

While the Japanese warplanes were still almost an hour away, two American soldiers on a small island in the Pacific scanned their radar and saw dots begin to fill their screen, representing the first wave of more than 180 bomber planes. The men notified their supervisor who, unfortunately, was an inexperienced novice. He shrugged off the situation with a ho-hum "don't worry about it."

Twenty-nine years earlier, a gargantuan, "unsinkable" ocean liner left her British port on her maiden voyage to New York. Just before midnight on April 14, 1912, the Titanic struck an iceberg. Two-and-a-half hours later the "unsinkable" vessel slipped beneath the icy waters with most of the passengers.

Such a large loss of life also didn't have to be. At the time of the disaster, less than 20 miles away and in sight of each other, another ship, the Californian, sat stationary in the Atlantic Ocean. With the time and capacity to save many hundreds of the Titanic's victims, what happened?

Someone on the Californian, who should have known better, ignored the potential for danger and simply decided to turn off the radio that night, resulting in the loss of 1,513 lives.

Here's the deal: Scripture exhorts us to "make the most of every opportunity" (Col. 4:5). As strange as it may sound, I believe disaster is coming to our shores to help bring us back to God. Yet in the face of America's imminent judgment (although probably not the final one), multitudes go on with business as usual, instead of readjusting priorities and better investing time to prepare for what's ahead.

Is it ultimately going to take a nightmarish calamity to jolt multitudes out of complacency and passivity in Christendom today? Remember Jonathan Edwards in America's first Great Awakening, who said that the primary hindrance to revival is spiritual pride, and nothing obliterates this vice like being humbled and brought to new dependence on God alone amidst a disaster. Remember Ps. 107:39: "Then their numbers decreased, and they were humbled by oppression, calamity and sorrow."

Fifteen "Signs of the Times" Indicating Judgment
The Bible warns us about saying "everything goes on as it has since the beginning of creation": (2 Pet. 3:4) when judgment is at hand. We know that God is "patient with you, not wanting anyone to perish" (v. 9), but there comes a time when the gavel falls!

After Hurricane Katrina, I spoke with a former resident of Louisiana. He told me that he grew up hearing warnings of levies breaking but folks simply tuned it out when nothing happened.

This describes America today.

If you fell asleep like a Rip Van Winkle for 30 years and awoke today, imagine how shocked you would be at what happened to America:

    1. Divorce: Increased from 4% to 51% in one generation.

2. Cohabitation: 65% of "altar-bound" couples "live together" (a euphemism for a lifestyle of fornication).

3. Abortion: 57 million unborn babies aborted, some with taxpayer funding and now part of socialized medicine.

4. Marijuana: Being legalized in certain states.

5. Euthanasia and Infanticide: Being legalized under camouflaged names.

6. Pornography: Rampant, graphic, just a "click away" on hand-held devices.

7. Homosexuality and transgender lifestyles: Promoted by even a U.S. President, along with gay marriage and homosexual ordinations.

8. Movies and music: Standards almost nonexistent, with graphic nudity, profanity, and blasphemy commonplace.

9. Out-of-wedlock births: For the first time in U.S history, they are at more than 50%.

10. Sexually transmitted diseases: Over 110 million Americans infected.

11. Economic insanity: almost $20 trillion national debt; 90 million unemployed and drawing government benefits; $60 billion in annual Medicare fraud and waste.

12. Illegal immigration: Over 11 million undocumented immigrants and politicians pushing open borders and amnesty.

13. Political leaders: Corruption, incompetence, and deception at all levels.

14. Radical Islam and terrorism: Exploding in regions of the world, with an increasingly vulnerable America dismantling militarily and docile politicians calling it a "peaceful religion."

15. Should we add illiteracy... crime... catastrophic fatherlessness... human trafficking... adultery... profane comedians... an ignorant and uninformed populace?

How about the ongoing erosion of our religious freedoms, and secularism taking over society?

And last, but not least, how about a Laodicean, apostate church, compromising and lacking the courage to address the defining issues of our day with clarity and conviction, while defining success in terms of happy sermons, attendance, offerings, number of staff, programs, and square footage?

Do we see the "handwriting on the wall" that we are at an unprecedented tipping point? Are we aware that America is rapidly spiraling into a lawless culture similar to the Germany of a generation ago?

My wife and her parents are German and they will tell you that an educated and civilized nation moved from democracy to dictatorship and then demise in less than six years! A once-thriving nation can have its heritage and faith so decimated that history records it as a tragic collapse.

Our Only Hope for Turnaround Is a Heaven-sent Awakening That May Require a Calamity to Jumpstart It

As long as things continue to run somewhat smoothly on the surface, we have an amazing ability to cope and carry on, all the while making flimsy excuses for compromise and a comfortable "Christianity":

- "I don't like what's happening in America on so many issues but it's not really affecting me or my family."

- "I prefer they not schedule sporting activities on Sunday morning but I guess we can live with it. As a family we try to make it to church at least twice a month, unless we need to catch up on our rest."

- "I wish our pastor would address these critical issues but he avoids controversy."

- "I grew up with Sunday school, Sunday evening, and Wednesday evening services but times have changed and I guess we can get by with a brief Sunday service."

- "Our worship leader is gay, I think, and the primary singer is living with her boyfriend but it's probably best not to stir up problems."

- "I wish our church gave out voter guides so we knew where candidates stand but since we're in a building program, leadership said they don't want to jeopardize fundraising."
- "Our pastors tell us they don't put out any lawn signs for candidates or speak about anything political because of separation of church and state."
- "We got the Evite for the citywide gathering to pray for transformation in our city but it's the same night as the *Dancing With the Stars* finale and we just can't miss it."

"I know your deeds, that you are neither cold nor hot. I wish you were either one or the other! So because you are lukewarm—neither hot nor cold—I am about to spit you out of my mouth. You say, 'I am rich; I have acquired wealth and do not need a thing.' But you do not realize that you are wretched, pitiful, poor, blind and naked."
(Revelation 3: 15-17)

Eight Potential Disasters to Awaken Us?

Will it take another stock-market crash, severe financial recession or, God forbid, global economic collapse to get our attention?

Might it take a series of beheadings and coordinated Islamic terrorist attacks in malls and cities by ISIS supporters slipping through unprotected borders to wake us up?

Would a massive power outage, shutting down computers and canceling NFL games nationwide, strike fear into the hearts of citizens and sober us to the urgency of the hour?

How about an airborne Ebola virus outbreak and the "pestilences and diseases" (Matthew 24:7) Jesus predicted at the end of the age? Maybe a mass migration of infected Central Americans streaming through our porous southern border?

Perhaps the beginning of war in the Middle East as enemies surround Jerusalem (Luke 21:20) and Iran launches "the bomb" on Israel, causing catastrophic disruption in the Straits of Hormuz (through which 20% of the total world's gas supply passes)? Recall the long gas lines of 1973?

Friends and family "handed over to be persecuted and put to death...hated by all nations because of Me" (Mt. 24:9)? Imagine us saying what a Chinese pastor, Huang Yizi, said this week upon being arrested in a government crackdown: "I am grateful to God for the opportunity to go to jail."

Perhaps the very real, dreaded, catastrophic EMP (electromagnetic pulse) attack causing unimaginable devastation by paralyzing America as all power lines burn out and all goes dark instantly? *USA Today* explained the potential situation thusly: "Cities darken, food spoils and homes fall silent. Civilization collapses." The cause: One terrorist A-bomb or a severe solar storm.

Massive earthquake(s), as Jesus foretold (Mt. 24:7). Scientist Dr. Lucy Jones issued a dire warning on October 15 to the L.A. City Council of the effects: "Infrastructure crippled; power grid and communications knocked out; water supply disrupted; 1,800 fatalities; 53,000 injured and one-half of the buildings unusable." (Note: This is *not* the inevitable "Big One" set for San Francisco.)

Awakening from a Spiritual Coma
After the disaster of 9/11, people flocked to church buildings, prayer meetings mushroomed, and streets were lined with marquees calling for God's blessing on America. We got our wake-up call and people were motivated to seek the living God as atheists and the ACLU were silenced.

Unfortunately, we hit the snooze button and fell back asleep. African pastors gathering in D.C. stated it this way: "America is in a spiritual coma!"

Providentially, during the same week over 100 churches gathered at the Lincoln Memorial in our nation's capital to cry out to God for one thing—spiritual awakening in the United States of America.

In the time of Esther, things looked bleak and God's people were very discouraged at the prospect of a national disaster. But through prayer, fasting, seeking God and Spirit-led action, God intervened to save the day. *"Who knows if you've come into the Kingdom for such a time as this?"* (Esther 4:14) was spoken over one believer. As the clock is ticking, can you hear God issuing you and me the same challenge?

Chapter 2
Perseverance

One Word Captures How Christians Continue Confidently Amidst Cultural Collapse–Perseverance

> *"Now may the God who gives perseverance and encouragement grant you to be of the same mind with one another according to Christ Jesus...."*
>
> *(Romans 15:5)*

Use your sanctified imagination to envision the following make-believe scenario:

Joel Osteen, Andy Stanley, Joyce Meyer, Ed Young Jr., Dave Ramsey, James Robison, Ken Copeland, Pat Robertson, Matt Crouch, and other high-profile Christian leaders all begin their programs with a sober warning, agreed upon in advance, to their collective millions of listeners:

> "The following message is completely uncharacteristic of our normal broadcast. But we are not living in normal times. We can't keep pretending God's judgments aren't real. What's happening currently can't be dismissed as coincidental but providential. We have come to the conclusion that God has directed leaders across this nation to simply communicate eight words: 'Forty more days and America will be destroyed.' That's what He instructed us to say. But there still is hope if we believe that God will have mercy on us, if we humbly turn back to Him and the ways of our Founding Fathers."

"Larry, that's unrealistic and too farfetched!"

"Do you know that the greatest awakening in world history took place when an obedient servant of God echoed those exact words in a different location? The leader and the people were so shaken by the severity of the message that they turned from their sinful ways and returned to God."

"When God saw what they did and how they turned from their evil ways, He had compassion and did not bring upon them the destruction He had threatened." (Read the entire account of this amazing, historical event in Jonah 3:3–10.)

What Will It Take to Awaken Us?

On an individual basis, scores of people say that their conversions took place after a series of events jolted them to humble themselves and turn to God. Should we not expect something similar for a nation at large? *"They were hungry and thirsty, and their lives ebbed away. Then they cried out to the Lord in their trouble and he delivered them from their distress."* (Psalm 107: 5-6)

An amalgam of unexpected, swift events exploding in tandem with each other would certainly get the attention of millions in America. The following are events within the realm of possibility very shortly: devastating economic collapse; horrific drought, gas and food shortages; war in the Middle East; a series of coordinated Islamic terrorist attacks; the outbreak of a new AIDS-like virus; racial riots erupting nationwide; multiple massive earthquakes; an Internet-crippling EMP attack; assassinations, and political chaos.

David Stockman, Ronald Reagan's former Budget Director, says of the economy, "All hell is about to break loose!"

ISIS just released a statement, as reported in *Charisma News*, that they have over seventy trained terrorists in fifteen U.S. states now.

To picture what it could be like when some of these events explode on the scene, picture a segment from the film *Mad Max* or the TV show *The Walking Dead* (I have not watched these but have seen pictures from them). Or visualize a city like those in the Ukraine—once-thriving cities now lawless centers of desperate people who've become marauders and looters carrying out criminal acts with impunity.

Our parents' generation exhibited patience, sacrifice, discipline and civility in difficult times. Being realistic (recall what happens when race riots erupt) and not dismissing all of this as nonsensical conspiracy theories, do we really expect people in a crisis today to let others go ahead of them in lines and for folks to patiently serve one another amidst shortages, curfews, and roving vigilantes?

"God hasn't given us a spirit of fear..." but it might wake people up to pause and ponder some of these coming realities. Just read afresh what Jesus said would be taking place prior to His Return.

How Should We Then Live?

In the 1960s, theologian and prophet Francis Schaeffer posed this question to Christians. Analyzing events in history and foretelling what was coming to our nation, he warned us of this implosion while calling us to engage our culture and beseech God for divine intervention.

Christians can no longer settle for "status quo" religion with neatly packaged, sanitized, inspirational programs and services while ignoring the epidemic of Christians being persecuted and Western civilization crumbling. In England, the former Archbishop of Canterbury said, "Christianity is facing extinction in Great Britain."

We are currently engaged in a titanic, unprecedented struggle with forces of evil and must categorically reject wishful thinking that this is simply temporary, cyclical, or manageable.

We are at a tipping point at which we will either experience a divine intervention of God in a Third Great Awakening or we will witness the fulfillment of A.W. Tozer's prophetic warning:

"Historians will conclude that we of the 20th century had the genius to create a great civilization but we lacked the moral wisdom to preserve it."

One Word Captures Our Charge

In Matthew 24 and Mark 13, Jesus told us the signs of the end of the age. He basically summed everything up with these words: "He who perseveres to the end will be saved" (Mt 24:13; Mk13:13). And in Romans 5:3 God tells us "... suffering produces perseverance."

There simply are no shortcuts in difficult days. We must draw upon the grace of God and make a quality decision that we will persevere.

Presently I'm reading a book, *The Churchill Factor: How One Man Made History*. This biography of the towering figure of the twentieth century who saved Western civilization from extinction demonstrated one overarching quality—perseverance.

When his fellow countrymen and Cabinet were capitulating to Hitler and his war machine, Winston Churchill told them to persevere, to fight, and to not negotiate. *"If this long island story of ours is to end at last, let it end only when each one of us lies choking in his own blood upon the ground!"* With this almost Shakespearean climax, he rallied them to press on until victory was theirs.

Days ago I spent some time with my wife in Oak Ridge, Tennessee, called the "Secret City" during World War II. Here 75,000 citizens worked tirelessly to develop the atomic bomb to ultimately defeat Japan and bring about its surrender. These patriots, alongside our servicemen and women who gave their lives on battlefields, and in the D-Day invasion, persevered to secure our freedom.

Recently, Supreme Court rulings may tip the scales in a way that may accelerate judgment on our land. May perseverance be our watchword. Remember the words of the prophet Jeremiah: *"If you have raced with men on foot and they have worn you out, how can you compete with horses? If you stumble in safe country, how will you manage in the thickets by the Jordan?"* (Jer. 12:5)

Our *Bullseye Challenge* launches with an emphasis on perseverance—*not* just personal perseverance in overcoming setbacks, but a collective call to *not* give up as we face incredible opposition, persecution, and adversity in the coming days.

Chapter 3
Ignorance

Persevere Amidst Cultural Ignorance

A popular feature of numerous TV shows is man-on-the-street interviews. You've probably coughed up your Doritos at the antics and answers displayed on episodes of *Watters' World* and others. Latte in one hand, and maybe an iPhone in the other, our wide-eyed respondents dart back and forth, stammer and stutter, then finally float their answer out with all the assurance of a third grader.

"Jesus, ah, was, ah, born in....China"?

"'The Star-Spangled Banner' was written by...not sure— Bono?"

"Yeah...Michelle Obama is married to Sir Paul McCartney!"

"Henry Ford invented the...the...lightbulb?"

"The Vietnam War ended when Lincoln signed the Emancipation Proclamation. No wait...when Reagan told them to tear down the Wall. Right?!"

Night after night, the willing participants elicit howls of laughter as they display their ignorance and humiliate themselves on national TV. Just don't tell anybody how many times you thought, "Sure glad I'm not the dude standing there looking like an idiot!"

As we read current surveys and review the testing results of millions of Americans—especially young people—the news is sobering, especially when it comes to knowledge of history, civics, and current affairs.

> *"If voters don't know what is going on in politics, they cannot rationally exercise control over government policy... Most individual voters are abysmally ignorant of even very basic political information."*
> —*Professor Ilya Somin*

Somin's depressing conclusion is being echoed today by scores of commentators, educators, social scientists, and concerned leaders in every field. When you consider the fact that, in a recent presidential election, eighty-three million eligible voters did NOT even cast a vote, maybe it's time to call "time out."

What's true for the general populace is actually worse when we zero in on the thirty-and-unders.

In his excellent book, *The Dumbest Generation (How the Digital Age Stupefies Young Americans and Jeopardizes Our Future),* [1] author Mark Bauerlein observes:

> *"...the intellectual future of the United States looks dim...the 70s joke about college students after late-60s militancy had waned still holds.*
>
> *'What do you think of student ignorance and apathy?' The interviewer asked the sophomore.*
>
> *"I dunno and I don't care."*
>
> *It isn't funny anymore. The Dumbest Generation cares little for history books, civic principles, foreign affairs, comparative religions, serious media and art, and it knows less."*

Bauerlein goes on to say that the ramifications for the United States are grave. If lessons in schools are watered down, if fewer books are read, if malls, movies, and media celebrities are more the focus than even a basic understanding of the issues and information shaping our world and the future—we're sinking into some deep doo-doo!

A few years ago, the Intercollegiate Studies Institute released their findings on the state of college students regarding civics (pssst: that's the study of the privileges and responsibilities of citizens). The results weren't pretty.

"The Coming Crisis in Citizenship: Higher Education's Failure to Teach America's History & Institutions" revealed...Are you ready?...College freshmen averaged an "F" on basic topics and the seniors...Are you ready? ...Ditto!

What's happened with young people? Research reveals the following:

- Twenty-two percent can name all five members of the Simpson cartoon family, yet only one in 1,000 can name all five First-Amendment freedoms (speech, religion, press, assembly, and redress of grievances).

- TV and video games now consume six to eight hours daily.

- YouTube and Facebook distract millions for gobs of time, night and day.

- Sixty-five percent aren't proficient in reading—even reading websites!

- Nine of the top ten sites youth are on are not educational—they're for social networking.

- Primary news sources consist of sound bites, on-screen scrolls, and *The Daily Show*.

- Cell-phone usage and texting are off the charts.

- Pop stars and their quirky lifestyles generate more interest than political issues.

- Only twenty percent of young Americans eighteen to thirty-four read a daily newspaper. They subsist on social media, scrolling headlines or sound-bite swatches sandwiched between celebrity breakups or breakdowns.

Cyber-culture has had disturbing effects on today's under-30s. The younger generation has all the advantages of technology: the

Internet's "information super-highway"; blogs; email; ultra-real and interactive video games; a vast array of cable options like the History Channel and the Discovery Channel; instant access to libraries, museums, and masterpieces worldwide; Internet connectivity; digital wonders; and virtual communities. They have all the opportunities to become the most enlightened generation in history.

Yet, the reality is that, instead of becoming an informed citizenry, the tendency is to milk the innovations to electronically exchange and download texts, tunes, trivialities, and today's latest photos or celebrity scoop.

"Is Google Making Us Stupid?"

This intriguing title was the cover story for the *Atlantic Monthly* magazine in August of 2008. Listen to some of the honest observations offered by the writer, Nicholas Carr:

> I've had an uncomfortable sense that someone, or something, has been tinkering with my brain, remapping the neural circuitry, reprogramming the memory. My mind isn't going— so far as I can tell—but it's changing. I'm not thinking the way I used to. I can feel it most strongly when I'm reading. Immersing myself in a book or a lengthy article used to be easy. My mind would get caught up in the narrative or the turns of the argument, and I'd spend hours strolling through long stretches of prose.

> That's really not the case anymore. Now my concentration starts to drift after two or three pages. I get fidgety, lose the thread, begin looking for something else to do. I feel as if I'm always dragging my wayward brain back to the text. The deep reading that used to come naturally has become a struggle.

Carr went on to describe how online research once took days—well now a few Google searches and wham-o—it's done!

The bottom line: The way Carr and millions of others are thinking has changed dramatically!

Do you identify? As your mind has tuned in to the information highway, complete with e-blasts, text crawls, pop-up ads, sound bites, bulleted articles, and easy-to-scan info-snippets, are you aware that this has catapulted you out from being more informed to less? We are sacrificing something and being drained of significant insights toward information critical to making decision and discerning issues for our future.

Voila! That's why this book was written, but it will take perseverance to complete the 30-day challenge. "Starting is easy. Sticking is hard."

Bullseye will give you a concise perspective on today's defining issues, along with common-sense principles for discovering solutions. Other books address these issues in a scholarly way (and that's good), but who's reading them? Oftentimes it's the pinheads, already convinced, or policy wonks and NOT the vast majority who need help without all the gobbledygook concepts and challenging terminology.

Albert Einstein said, "Make everything as simple as possible, but no simpler." We'll employ "brief and amazing" videos and articles absorbing thirteen minutes, followed by two minutes of prayerful reflection. Do it for thirty days to become an informed influencer.

So let's persevere until we complete the task! We'll follow the K.I.S.S. formula—Keep It Simple Sweetie!

May the Bullseye Challenge help us eradicate some of our stupidity and enable us to think clearly about today's core issues.

Chapter 4
Truth

Persevere Amidst Deviation From Truth

It's a hot and humid summer evening, yet the enjoyment of the sights and sounds of the old ballpark eclipse any discomfort you feel. Nestled in your seat, surrounded by friends, you grab a few more goo-ified nachos and sip your Dr. Pepper.

Suddenly the gentle stirring, standing, and stretching begins. The melodic organ music kicks in as you remember, "Oh yeah, it's time for our summertime serenade, 'Take Me Out to the Ball Game!'" You jostle your goodies and stand to your feet, ready for the time-honored, seventh-inning stretch.

Wait! Whoever started this summertime tradition, repeated nightly all over America?

Somewhere back in 1910 at a baseball game in the nation's capital between the Washington Senators and the Athletics, our 300-pound 27th President of United States, William Howard Taft, stood up in the middle of the seventh inning. People dressed more formally in those days so, understandably, he was hot and most uncomfortable in his cramped wooden chair.

Thinking he was about to exit, the rest of the crowd respectfully stood as well. It was a sort of an early "wave" experience. It concluded when he returned his rump to the chair.

The change of position obviously proved beneficial as it was repeated in a subsequent game, along with the later addition of the catchy tune. A tradition was born, thanks to a portly president who probably never knew he was the catalyst for this now-106-year-old routine.

Today, after America's 400-year journey as a nation, we need to persevere and also participate in a collective seventh-inning stretch. Let's stand and begin.

It would do us well to not merely pause, take a deep breath, then dig back in for more bickering, bashing, attacking, and mocking of politicians and pundits over differing views. America is divided on many fronts, although we are united on at least one thing—more than 80 percent of us agree that our country is headed in the wrong direction!

Like those who partied on the Titanic, many Americans are unaware of the disaster looming ahead. Multitudes seem to be asleep or in some sort of fog.

In 2008, Russian literary giant Alexander Solzhenitsyn passed away. Some of us may recall his commencement address at Harvard University in 1978, in which he warned us about many of today's cultural ills. Challenging us to steer clear of the abandonment of our Christian heritage and recover our adherence to the Supreme Being who "used to restrain our passions and irresponsibility," this brilliant prophet spoke words we need to heed afresh during these turbulent times.

The Summer of Love

To understand our nation's cultural decline, we need to rewind the tape to a pivotal time—the 1960s—to discover how our free fall started. Beginning with the shocking assassination of President Kennedy, a flickering of Camelot—inspired hope was extinguished. Prayer and Bible reading were banned from our public schools and the "God is dead" pronouncement of 1966 fostered an era of skepticism and cynicism bleeding through our land.

It's not as if there was one defining event that triggered our current confusion, but when the turbulent twenty-four months of '67 and '68 erupted on the scene, clues emerged. Cultural analysts call this a "tipping point."

The summer of 1967 was dubbed the "Summer of Love." Scores of us naïve youth fell in line behind pied piper Scott McKenzie as we grabbed our knucklehead buddies and love beads and swayed with the wind all the way to San Francisco. Do you remember the song? "If you going to San Francisco/You're going to meet some gentle people there…All across the nation, there's a new generation… People in motion, people in motion." For those who do remember, it almost moves you to put some flowers in your hair!

Millions of us idealistic young people and our hippie friends believed we were ushering in the long-awaited "Age of Aquarius" with all our peace symbols, free love, and free speech. American psychologist Timothy Leary took LSD and told us, "Turn on, tune in, and drop out." Seduced by our foolishness we declared, "Never trust anyone over 30!" while Pete Townshend of the Who exclaimed, "Hope I die before I get old!" (He's over 70 and still cashing in on his musical career!) Soon thereafter, hundreds of thousands were sloshing in the mud at the Woodstock Festival—can you believe it's been almost fifty years?

Jim Morrison, lead singer of the Doors, was my idol. I even did a college term paper on his life entitled "The Amplified Poet." His moronic philosophy: "I'm interested in anything about revolt, disorder, chaos, especially activities that appear to have no meaning. It seems to me to be the road to freedom!"

Slowly but surely, those of us who "sowed the wind–reaped the whirlwind," as the Bible teaches in Hosea 8:6. Years of supposed freedom began to take its toll. The good times began to sour and bite us in the butt! TIME Magazine called 1968 "a knife blade that severed past from the future."

Casting off restraints to protest and launch the gay, women's and Black Power movements, the sexual revolution and the drug counterculture, we soon morphed into meltdown. The Civil Rights Movement was a positive initiative, but not everyone was going "Hoop Dee Doo" about it.

In just a few years, pop idols Janis Joplin, Jimi Hendrix, and Jim Morrison all were dead at age twenty-seven–overdosing on drugs, sex, and unrestrained freedom. Sexually transmitted diseases started breaking out everywhere. AIDS (or GRID—Gay-related immune deficiency, as it was called in the beginning) soon followed. Bobby Kennedy and Martin Luther King Jr. were assassinated. Student riots paralyzed Chicago. The Altamont Rock Festival degenerated into murderous mayhem right before Mick Jagger's bloodshot eyes. One hour from where I attended college, Kent State University erupted in campus shootings over the still-simmering Vietnam War. Hippie communities and gay bathhouses started folding like houses of cards as Barry McGuire sang his number-one hit, "Eve of Destruction." Abortion demands intensified as all the "Make love, not war," mantras spawned unwanted babies—conveniently called "unwanted products of conception" to mask the guilt and deceive millions. Soon abortion was legalized, resulting in almost 59 million unborn babies' lives being terminated—the eradication of about one third of the entire generation born since 1973!

Divorce laws were liberalized (today eighty percent of divorces are "no fault," translating into 45 million divorces since the end of the 1960s!). Sexual standards evaporated and resulted in rampant pornography, skyrocketing out-of-wedlock births, one in every four teens strapped with a sexually transmitted disease, drug abuse, school violence, teen suicide, spousal and child abuse, violent crime, prison overpopulation, sexual anarchy, gender confusion, glamorizing and promotion of homosexuality and bisexuality, and transgenderism with gender reassignment surgeries. All of this proliferated since the now infamous "Summer of Love" soured to a stench. And surveys today celebrate how "progressive "America is becoming as we discard traditional ways.

Dr. James Dobson, famous author and family advocate, identified six lies that have taken root in the United States:

1. Premarital, extramarital, and traditionally abnormal sex are moral and healthy.

2. There should be no sanctity of human life in law.

3. Drug use makes great recreational sport.

4. Divorce offers an easy escape from marriage.

5. Marriage should be redefined to include same-sex unions.

6. God is dead—at least make it appear that way by systematically airbrushing Him from society.

Dobson asks, "Can anyone seriously deny that these ideas have wreaked havoc on our society over the four decades since they gained prominence?"

As we proceed with the Bullseye Challenge, we must realize what is at stake for our families and our future. If you are a young person understanding this information for the first time, it's critical you realize what has happened and you take a courageous stand and become informed on the critical issues so you can make a difference in reversing this dangerous direction.

Multitudes of people need a reality check to bring them out of a sentimental yet distorted remembrance of this period. We must remove the romantic recollections of the turbulent 1960s. In contrast to PBS's nostalgic specials highlighting the supposedly peaceful and musical hippie era, we need to come down to earth and recognize the devastation that resulted. This was not a time that was all groovy, lovey, and peaceful, with flowing hair, girls in granny dresses twirling in the park amidst syrupy-faced guys with tambourines and doves flying around their heads as they harmonized in childlike unity, singing "Kumbaya" and playing flutes while innocently getting high. This is a demonic illusion and a fantasy that needs to be shattered immediately. Don't be taken in!

Here's the deal: we have veered terribly off the path of our Founding Fathers. Robert Hunt consecrated this nation to God at its founding when he planted a cross on Virginia Beach in April 1607. The truth from the Bible upon which our nation was established has been distorted and discarded. The crisis we are presently in is simply a crisis of truth.

The Crisis of Truth in America
Simply stated, here's the downward spiral we're experiencing—the pattern repeated throughout history:

- Reject truth

- Lose discernment

- Moral confusion

Rome, one of the greatest civilizations of all time, followed this downward path leading to destruction. Likewise, Germany went from democracy to dictatorship to demise in six years, basically plummeting along this same path. The apostle Paul was used by God to warn people of this pattern when he wrote his divinely inspired masterpiece to the Roman people:

> *The wrath of God is being revealed from heaven against all the godlessness and wickedness of men who suppress the truth [reject truth]...although they knew God, they neither glorified Him as God nor gave Him thanks, but their thinking became futile and their foolish hearts were darkened [lose discernment]...They exchanged the truth of God for a lie... Because of this, God gave them over to...[What follows is a cascading list of behaviors including shameful homosexual behavior, perversion, greed, deceit, envy, murder, strife, arrogance, dishonoring parents, and inventing ways of doing evil (moral confusion)]" (See Romans 1:18–32).*

Although it's not pleasant, it's really not that complicated! The insightful words of humorist Mark Twain have particular relevance here: "Most people are bothered by those passages in Scripture which they cannot understand; but as for me, I always notice that the passages in Scripture which trouble me most are those I do understand!"

As multitudes today cry out for social justice, isn't it plain as the nose on our face that we should be waving a red flag before it's too late? Consider just one area—so-called unrestrained sexual freedom. Because of dishonoring sexual purity before marriage and fidelity in marriage, along with pornography, homosexuality, and skyrocketing out-of-wedlock births, plus the soaring epidemic of STDs and AIDS, we have lost the lives of nearly 59 million little babies who have been exterminated in the womb. That's more than the combined populations of Atlanta, Boston, Chicago, Dallas, Denver, Detroit, Houston, Los Angeles, Miami, Minneapolis, New Orleans, New York, Philadelphia, Phoenix, San Francisco, Seattle, St. Louis and Washington DC combined! Something is terribly wrong with this picture.

Two thousand years ago, a Roman governor named Pilate asked Jesus Christ, "What is truth?"

His response revealed the simple mission for which Jesus Christ said He came into the world: "I came into the world to testify to the truth" (Jn 18:37-38). He also said, "I am the Way the Truth and the Life" (Jn 14:6).

Isn't it wonderful to know that we not only follow the embodiment of all truth, but that we can be His ambassadors to charitably and courageously communicate it to our generation? In a world putting forth false ideals of plurality and neutrality and diversity, our mission is to make a difference by persevering through these dark days to learn the truth, model the truth, and make it known to everyone we can.

Let's conclude by imagining the following scenario:
    At the end of time, billions of people were scattered on a great plain before God's throne. Some of the groups near the front talked angrily.
    "How can God judge us? How can He know about suffering?" screamed a cynical brunette, as she jerked back a sleeve to reveal a tattooed number from a Nazi concentration camp. "We endured terror, beatings, torture, and death!"
    In another group, a black man lowered his collar. "What about this?" he demanded, showing an ugly rope burn. "Lynched for no crime but being black! We have suffocated in slave ships, been wrenched from loved ones and toiled 'til only death gave release."
    "What about our group? Radical Islamists tortured us in the name of Allah, kidnapped our wives and daughters, and then savagely and barbarically took our lives! Over the centuries they forced us to convert to Islam or risk being beheaded!"
    Far out across the plain were hundreds of such oppressed peoples. Each had a complaint against God for the evil and suffering He permitted in the world. "How lucky God was to live in heaven where there was no repression. All was sweetness and light. No weeping, no fear, no hunger, no hatred. Indeed, what did God know about the hassles man had in this world? After all, God leads a pretty sheltered life."
    So each group sent out a leader, chosen because he had suffered the most. There was a Jew, a black man, a martyr, an untouchable from India, an illegitimate son, a prisoner of war, an American Indian, and many from slave camps. In the center of the plain they consulted with each other. At last they were ready to present their case. It was rather simple—before God would be qualified to be their judge, He must endure what they had endured. Their decision was that God should be sentenced to live on earth—as a man!
    They came up with a Top 10 list He must fulfill. And to level the playing field, He must set aside all divine powers to help Himself.

    1. Let him be born a Jew!

2. Let the legitimacy of his birth be doubted so that no one will know who his father really is.

3. Let him champion a cause so just, but so radical, that it brings down upon him the hatred, condemnation, and eliminating efforts of the establishment and every major religious authority.

4. Let him be the object of putdowns and ridicule, be spat upon and labeled "demon" and "mad "even though his character is impeccable and his life is devoted to helping the downtrodden, poor, and sick."

5. Let him try to describe what no one has ever seen, touched, heard or smelled—let him try to communicate God.

6. Let him be betrayed by his dearest friends and abandoned by those closest to him.

7. Let him be indicted on false charges, tried before a prejudiced jury, then convicted by a cowardly judge even though he never committed sin or a crime.

8. Let him experience what it is to be terribly alone and almost completely abandoned in his greatest time of need.

9. Let him be tortured, stripped naked, and then left to die a humiliating, unbelievable death.

10. And let his name live on so that for centuries it will be used as a common curse word in moments of rage.

As each leader announced his portion of the sentence, loud murmurs of approval went up from the great throng of people. When the last had finished pronouncing sentence, there was a long silence. No one uttered another word. No one moved. For suddenly they all knew...

God already served his sentence.

The gospel is the good news that God became a man in Jesus Christ and lived a sinless life, then died in our place the death we should have died as rightful judgment for our sins. He rose from the dead on the third day just as He said, proving He was God and offering forgiveness of sin, and abundant and eternal life to all who repent and put their trust in Him as Lord and Savior.

As we continue our journey, if you have never asked God to forgive you of your sins and then put your trust in Him alone to be your Lord and Savior, do it now. Then let's persevere together as a team going forward to bring the truth to our lost and confused world.

Chapter 5
Worldview: Secular or Spiritual?

Perspective: What Is Your Worldview?

Ten blind people, each feeling a different part of an elephant, will describe the creature differently because of one thing—perspective. The same holds true when approaching "hot-button" issues in our culture today. What is the lens through which we are looking?

How would you like to be awakened one morning to discover someone is suing you for $22 million? It happened to me years ago because I said in a speech that the author of the bestseller *I'm OK, You're OK* took his life. I heard this interesting tidbit from a man who heard it from an internationally known Christian leader but they were dead wrong (no pun intended)! My perspective was faulty and I suffered through an agonizing four-year ordeal before a breakthrough came.

Remember humorist Mark Twain's classic line upon reading his erroneous obituary one morning in the newspaper? "The reports of my untimely death have been greatly exaggerated." If only the late Dr. Harris had found my mishap so funny!

All of my traumatic experiences came because of a wrong perspective. That's why having the right perspective is so critical in life's journey.

How about you? Are there some areas in your life where your perspective may be skewed or, dare we say, dead wrong? As you continue with the Bullseye Challenge be prepared to make course corrections so you are more informed and accurate about important issues facing us in our nation today.

Contrary to what many in our culture propagate, here are the three realities of a worldview that will bring you stability, success, and security in life:

1. Truth exists and is knowable.

2. Truth upheld brings blessings.

3. Truth disregarded brings consequences.

A biblical worldview is not based upon subjective experiences, popularity polls, or the shifting sands of public opinion. Rather it is firmly grounded in objective, absolute truth—"true truth." It is unchanging, timeless, and rock-solid in make-up, unlike so much of what comes our way in culture today. So many of our cultural problems result from the fact that the moral compass that formerly guided us in this nation has been shattered by many in the pursuit of pleasure and personal fulfillment.

I'm challenging you to make a quality decision to center your life upon divine revelation, not man's speculation. Charles Darwin, in *Origin of Species* (the basis for much of the teaching of evolution in schools today), repeated over and over, "Let us assume." I, for one, don't want to base my life on assumption, but rather on God's timeless revelation.

Not long ago a senator with presidential ambitions saw his campaign come to a screeching halt. While he was married to a wonderful woman who was battling cancer, John rationalized that it was okay to commit adultery on the side. When asked about it on national television, he flat-out lied regarding the affair. A man of real integrity, huh?

His "lover" was a divorced party girl who was steeped in New Age spirituality. She was a "firm believer in the power of truth" and "fiercely devoted to astrology." She also believed in reincarnation, that she had led "many lives" and that souls enter and escape a "field of consciousness."

This deceived woman believed she knew truth. She had a perspective but, boy, was it wacko! In the end she and he destroyed his marriage, the wife divorced him and died, the children suffered, and his campaign collapsed on the national stage. To this day he remains a laughingstock for his stupidity and will carry to the grave his aspirations that flamed out on the bed of illusion and lust.

We are surrounded in our culture by many people who like to call themselves "progressives" and "postmodern." They believe that there is no such thing as objective truth. They want to free society from "rigid "categories and "fixed" meanings for a more subjective approach to life. "What I experience as true is true for me," they might say. So if I believe that I was born a man but I'm really a woman or that multiple marriage partners united together is the best way to be happy or that having intimate relations as an adult man with a 12-year-old boy is my sexual preference and orientation, who are you to say it's wrong? Truth is what works for you!

We want to help bring about transformation in our society through a restoration of truth being communicated in a winsome yet uncompromising way. The Bible tells us to "speak the truth in love." Truth without love leads to legalism—gaining acceptance with God by performance. Love without truth leads to licentiousness—anything goes because God forgives.

Forty-five years ago I made a quality decision to base all of my life and the decisions of life upon what the Bible says, not what people think it says or twists it to say. The result of honoring scripture has been a marriage of almost forty years (my wife's parents are seventy years married!), plus wonderful children and grandchildren. We discovered a life of purpose, joy, peace, and security by obeying God's holy Word.

It's sad to say, but there is so much illiteracy in our country when it comes to the Bible. Barna Research found the following:

- Fifty-eight percent of people surveyed don't know who preached the Sermon on the Mount.

- Forty-eight percent of all adults don't know that the Book of Thomas is not in the Bible.

- Seventy percent of adults didn't know that the expression "God helps those who help themselves" is not in the Bible. The expression originally came from Ben Franklin!

It really is time to gain a better understanding of the Bible as not primarily some harsh, legalistic code of dos and don'ts but rather as a guidebook of timeless wisdom for God's glory and our good! It also provides us with a coherent framework for outlining society's problems and the remedy for them. Just ask the hundreds of thousands of people who have been liberated from the shackles of debt by applying Dave Ramsey's Biblical guidance on finances. Maybe Congress needs to apply these principles!

Our challenge is simple: will we follow a secular or a scriptural worldview? Remember, for best results, follow the instructions in the manufacturer's handbook. This does take humility, something that seems in short supply in so many people's lives today. May this simple chart help us see the two pathways before us.

Contrasting Secular and Scriptural Worldviews

- *Scriptural*: according to Biblical wisdom and principles
- *Secular*: from the Latin "*saeculum*" (time or age), focused on this age alone, rejecting religion and eternity
- *Worldview*: how you view all of life, the lens through which you view reality, your personal belief system—WHAT PATH ARE YOU PURSUING?

ISSUE	SECULAR VIEW	SCRIPTURAL VIEW
Truth	Subjective and experimental (what feels right)	Revealed and knowable, one divine source, objective
The Bible	An old, religious book with stories and insights	Revealed will of God for all areas of life
The Universe & History	Evolution- and man-centered	Creation- and God-centered
Man's Condition	Inherently good, improving to a higher state	Sinful makeup requires redemption
Source of Problems	Ignorance or environment (sees self as victim)	Human sinfulness (take responsibility for own actions)

ISSUE	SECULAR VIEW	SCRIPTURAL VIEW
God	Whoever, whatever, or denial	Loving Creator, merciful Savior, righteous Judge
Plight	Ignorant of potential (evolving)	Separated from God (spiritually dead)
Sin	Disregarded or redefined as addiction	Choices, disobeying God
Solution	Legislation, education, therapy	Regeneration (a spiritual "rebirth")
Provision	Education, science, technology	The gospel—Person and finished work of Jesus Christ
Jesus	Moral teacher & example	Son of God, Lord & Savior
Response	Improve through effort, spiritual activities	Yield to God—repent, trust and obey
Guilt	Conditioned response	Conviction to lead to confession/change
Accountability	Optional or for "serious" offenders	All responsible for choices
Responsibility	Codependent victims	Everyone responsible for choices
Orientation	Serve self, demand "rights," embrace entitlements	Please God, live humbly; serve others
Change	Excuse, shift blame, plead ignorance, rationalize behavior	Follow Bible, mature in character
Afterlife	Denied, ignored, reincarnation, annihilation	Enter God's presence (heaven) or eternal separation (hell)
Judgment	Non-existent or avoided by "good works"	Disobedience punished & obedience rewarded by a just and loving God
Goal of Life	Personal pleasure, self-fulfillment, acquisition of wealth & possessions	Glorify God, fulfill destiny, serve humanity, enjoy eternity

Consider statements from two individuals with different worldviews. Think of their lives and what legacy they left.

>*"All there is is nature and humanity."*
>—Karl Marx, founder of communism (which destroyed about one hundred million lives)

>*"When people stop believing in God, they don't believe in nothing—they believe in anything."*
>—G. K..Chesterton, prolific author and world-renowned literary influencer for Christ

Chapter 6
Godless vs. God Bless America

Separation of Church and State?
"Larry, I'm an atheist! I don't believe in God. Now if there is a God, He could appear to me and walk in this room and then I would probably believe. But I don't believe there is any God and of that I am certain."

When someone says something like the above to me, here's what I usually do. I take a piece of paper and a pen and I draw a large circle. Then I ask the person, "If the circle represents all the knowledge there is in all the world, what percentage would you believe represents the amount of knowledge you have?" Do they know ten percent of all there is to know in the universe? Do they know twenty-five percent? Then I draw a slice inside the circle that represents that percentage.

Not in a smart-alecky way, but in a respectful way, I then point to the remaining percentage of the circle. "Jim, if you know about twenty percent of all there is to know and you admit there is about eighty percent that you do not know, is it possible in that 80% there's a chance God might exist?"

If the conversation is pleasant, my experience, in forty years of engaging people like this, is that most will admit it's possible. Then I gently say that what best describes their mentality is one of being an agnostic rather than an atheist. In other words, God might exist but they don't know for sure. Progress has been made and I encourage everyone who tries this to continue this dialogue over the months until the person reaches a greater time of need. My wife said she was an atheist until her world began to crumble; then she started to look up to the living God!

Jesus told "Doubting Thomas" in the Bible, "Because you have seen me, you have believed; blessed are those who have not seen and yet have believed" (Jn 20:29). Our challenge is to reach those who have not seen and help them discover the living God. Remember: your life is the only Bible that many people will ever read!

Now Jesus told us that we are the "salt of the earth" (preserving from decay) and the "light of the world" (shedding light in darkness.). Scripture further tells us, "When the righteous are in authority, the people rejoice. When the wicked rule, the people groan" (Prv 29:2).

If Christians such as Dr. Martin Luther King Jr., Chuck Colson, William Wilberforce, Mother Teresa, George Washington, Abe Lincoln, George Washington Carver, and scores of others had backed off their Christian witness in the face of atheistic opposition and abdicated praying and participating in changing the culture for good, can you imagine the state of our world? Yet today there are individuals who advocate people of faith stay out of public affairs. They also believe passionately that God should be removed from the public square and mention of Him should be consigned to the inside of a church building or synagogue.

Authentic and courageous Christians respectfully disagree. We believe that engaging people in the marketplace and the political process to protect unborn babies, uphold the sanctity of marriage, speak up for social justice, and help persuade people to discover new life in Christ is our privilege and sacred responsibility. In a civil and winsome way we want to persuade individuals there is a better path than secularism; plus it is God, not us, who declares, "The fool says in his heart, 'There is no God'" (Ps. 14:1).

Religion-Free Zone?
"In the beginning God…" (Gen.1:1). These four words launch the first of sixty-six books in the best-selling book of all time, the holy Bible. What better way to begin than right here, especially since we

live in a country where ninety-six percent of its citizens say they believe in God?

When astronaut Buzz Aldrin stood on the surface of the moon decades ago, he gasped at the galaxy and let loose these familiar words into the expanse of the universe: "The heavens declare the glory of God, the skies proclaim the work of His hands" (Ps.19:1). He was acknowledging God's existence and His role as Creator, just as our Founding Fathers did in the beginning of the Declaration of Independence.

Today in America, there exists a small yet vocal and well-financed minority of individuals whose primary goal is to remove any reference to God from the public square and reshape our country into a religion-free zone. Known as "secularists" (focus on this word alone, which means to reject any forms of religion), or "secular progressives" along with those who now call themselves the "New Atheists" (rejecting any existence of God), they are on a mission to remove Judeo–Christian heritage from our nation, deceive the unsuspecting and advance their agenda in any way possible.

Articulate advocates of the "New Atheism" are Oxford evolutionary scholar Richard Dawkins, author of the New York Times bestseller *The God Delusion* and the late freelance thinker Christopher Hitchens, as well as Sam Harris. Their "beef" comes from the post-9/11 sense that religious fanaticism is a luxury the world can't afford any longer. Dawkins states that religious instruction is a form of child abuse and when asked about the origin of life, suggests that maybe aliens from outer space arrived to get the ball rolling. Imagine: extraterrestrials may have actually sparked life on our planet as we know it!

Richard Dawkins stated in TIME Magazine his views on good and evil: "Good and evil—I don't believe there is hanging out there anywhere something called good and something called evil." Understand that, when we dismiss the notion of God, we also need to dismiss truth since everything is relative or subjective. And if there is no truth then there is no basis for morality—something completely contrary to the Bible and our Founders who clearly communicated that our rights and laws were based on "Nature's God."

Comedian George Carlin, who died a few years ago at the age of seventy-one (he boasted that he was going to live until he was

ninety!), stated his atheistic philosophy like this: "For those of you
who look to the Bible for moral lessons and literary qualities, I
might suggest a couple of other stories for you. You might want
to look at 'The Three Little Pigs.' That's a good one... I've often
drawn a great deal of moral comfort from 'Humpty Dumpty!' The
part I like the best: 'All the king's horses and all the king's men
couldn't put Humpty Dumpty back together again.' That's because
there is no Humpty Dumpty and there is no God! None. Not one. No
God. Never was!"

When people say there is no God and/or no such thing as absolute
objective truth, we are then left with theory and therapy, which
characterizes much of America today. A recent survey stated that
sixty-three percent of Americans and only eight percent of teenagers
believe there is something called absolute, moral truth. See why we
have our work cut out for us?

No absolute truth? Let me bring a pizza delivery to your door
and withhold the scrumptious delight, saying that you didn't pay
when you did. "Hey, that's a lie! It'll always be a lie if you try that!"

Or witness someone strap on a bomb to kill innocent children.
"That is murder! It is always murder!"

How about observing someone shove your frail and disabled
grandparent out of the grocery store line to steal his or her place in
line. "That's stealing! That's taking their spot! It's always wrong!"

I thought there were no absolutes? Might they be absolutely
wrong?

What's happened in America since the 1960s should be our
wake-up call, lest we slide further down the slippery slope like other
places who have gone before us in decline. Let's take one example:
Quebec, Canada.

In the 1960s, something labeled the "Quiet Revolution" swept
through Quebec. In a relatively short period, the people abandoned
their Judeo-Christian values and embraced their "new morality."
Today, these are the facts: of all the Canadian provinces, Quebec has
the lowest marriage and birth rate and the highest abortion, divorce,
and suicide rates, and the churches are overwhelmingly barren in
what once was a strong Catholic center. (Sound like much of Europe
today?) And its sister city, Montreal, has become a notorious "haven
for pedophiles" according to Canada's leading news magazine.

One of history's greatest philosophers was the brilliant leader Blaise Pascal. He once said that "If there is no God and you bet your life there is, you've lost nothing. But if there is a God, and you bet your life there isn't, you've made the greatest mistake imaginable." Ever ponder the expression on the faces of people like John Lennon, George Carlin, Karl Marx, and others when they died and met their Maker? Well, there's always the chance of a deathbed conversion before they passed from this life.

A highly dedicated champion of the secularists is a multigazillionaire named George Soros. He's the leader of "MoveOn.org" and releases his resources for candidates and causes. to move on his vision of a "new America" similar to that of Europe's Amsterdam. Make no mistake about it; he is powerful and passionate in this pursuit and he's not alone. There are scores of politicians, celebrities, journalists, authors, and entertainers who all play on his type of team. Be alert!

As we continue our journey together, let's pause and ask ourselves what is so bad about trying to change America so it's more like the tranquil land of the windmills and wooden shoes. The Dutch are very nice, peaceful people, aren't they?

Having been to Amsterdam numerous times, let me take you there while tying in its significance for this defining moment in our nation's history. We really are at a crossroads and the sooner we realize it, the better!

If We Snooze—We Will Lose!

Awhile back, I was going to the airport in a van when a twenty-something young man seated behind me related the following account of his pregnant wife's recent death. "While driving home, I simply dozed for a few seconds. Rebounding, I found myself drifting into the next lane and then it was too late! The truck hit her side and I lost the love of my life... and our first child."

Tragedies happen. Some can be prevented; others can't. Wisdom dictates vigilance. In perilous times, it's imperative that we don't let our guard down, especially as it relates to the direction of our nation. "If we snooze—we will lose."

Amsterdam, Holland was the launch pad for our nation. Remember where our first settlers came from? The Dutch explorer Hudson first came to New York—initially called "New Netherlands." New York City was "New Amsterdam." Brooklyn, Harlem, the Hudson—they all derive their names from our ancestors. And what was Holland known for then, which continues today?

Tolerance
Now tolerance historically meant "respect for others' beliefs." Today it's evolved to mean "respect for others' behavior." In other words, there is no absolute standard of morality. "Every man does what is right in his own eyes" (Judg. 17:6).

Where can this approach lead? In Amsterdam, these are now legal realities:

- Abortion on demand
- Euthanasia—mercy killing or "death with dignity"
- Forms of infanticide
- Same-sex marriage
- Recreational drugs—hundreds of coffee shops selling hashish with different coffees
- Sex shows and open, explicit pornography right out on the street
- Open prostitution—27,000 "registered" ladies sit in sidewalk display windows
- Explicit homosexual, bisexual, and transvestite activity
- Public nudity
- Sex-change operations or "gender reassignment surgery"—subsidized by tax dollars
- Age of consent for sexual activity: twelve years of age
- "Burnout"—a paid "leave of absence" from work for extended periods, which is rampant and financed by tax dollars; most can draw their full salary during this time and can renew in five-year cycles

Let's stop and amplify just one of the above: euthanasia. In the Netherlands, the law on euthanasia is not limited to adults, nor does an applicant for euthanasia have to be terminally ill. The Netherlands plans to extend its existing euthanasia law for infants born with malformations. "It's very difficult to avoid this debate," says Jacqueline Herremans, president of the Association for the Right to Die with Dignity. "People are feeling, 'Who is the master of my life? It is not God. It's not the state. It's not the physician. I am the master of my life. And I'm the one to decide if I have to suffer or not.'"

In Europe, take Germany for example (where they should know better after Nazi eugenics programs killed more than 70,000 physically and mentally challenged people before and during World War II), where a doctor can supply a willing person with lethal drugs to kill himself if he so chooses. A person doesn't have to be in chronic pain or even be suffering from a terminal illness. He or she may simply not want to be moved to a nursing home. He or she may also be coached by greedy or unscrupulous relatives to "get this thing over with." Think about it: this could happen in America if we continue down this path. Canada already has "death panels" along these lines! Is this what you would want for your life? The potential is chilling.

The American Civil Liberties Union
Undergirding secularists and atheists, in their goal of a godless America, is the ACLU. Founded in 1920 by Roger Baldwin and Crystal Eastman, who had strong communist involvement, the ACLU works relentlessly towards its goal of dismantling and reshaping America into its godless image.

They march in lockstep, using legal intimidation and mis-information to declare that Christianity and Judaism and any religious influence must go! Consider a handful of causes they promote:

- Removing even "moments of silence," pregame voluntary prayer, and graduation invocations.
- Stopping any religious symbolism on any public property
- Defending distribution of child pornography and removing laws to protect children from registered sex offenders

- Promoting acceptance of and education about homosexual behavior in schools while opposing any dissent to Darwinian evolutionary theory or free debate regarding Intelligent Design/Creationism
- Overturning the bedrock institution of male/female marriage to radically redefine marriage and family along same-sex lines
- Allowing Wiccan witches to open town meetings with their mystical, humanistic "prayer" while blocking attempts by Christians and Jews.
- Forcing Boy Scouts and Girl Scouts to accept gays and lesbians as scout leaders.

People need to realize the nature of this organization that works aggressively to marginalize biblical values, undermines parental authority, removes protection for our children from predators and pornographers, and undercuts the sanctity of human life from conception to natural death.

Separation of Church and State
"What about our Constitution's mandate to be tolerant and uphold the 'wall of separation between church and state?' I get tongue-tied all the time when I try to state something and people just throw this in my face!"

You must understand that secularists are working for two primary goals:

1. To convey the idea that our Founding Fathers intended America to be free from religion—separated by a wall between church and state—so that any religious influence in government and schools must be silenced.

2. To convey the idea that the origins of our country came not from Judeo-Christian adherents but rather a mishmash of agnostics, deists, atheists, and greedy opportunists who came here for material gain and to displace the Native Americans.

Here's the deal: both of these positions are absolutely false! They are myths! Don't be deceived—push the delete button now. If you are in a school where this propaganda is being implanted into the classroom, stop your ears!

First, our Constitution was designed to give us freedom of religion—not freedom from religion. That's why the early settlers fled religious persecution in England to come here in the first place. They wanted no state church, unlike what they had in England. They had faced considerable government interference in England; this was something they wanted to free themselves from as they came to America.

Second, the phrase "wall of separation between church and state" is nowhere to be found in the Constitution! It comes from a letter by Thomas Jefferson to the Danbury Baptists in 1802, assuring them of a First Amendment "wall" preventing government from interfering with religion or denying people's right to freely exercise their religion.

Third, let it be known to those striving to reconstruct an America separate from our authentic Judeo-Christian heritage, it's time to reaffirm our origins and honor the faith of our forebears. It was Aristotle who said, "If you would understand anything, observe its beginning and its development."

Finally, tolerance does not translate into believing that every view is equal, but rather respecting others' right to hold different views, though they may be terribly wrong (say, if they believe in the tooth fairy or the Loch Ness monster hoax!). All ideas can have equal hearing while not having equal footing. And we must have the courage to compassionately communicate truth, based on divine revelation, instead of some namby-pamby, politically correct, offend nobody, so just stay silent approach.

Bullseye! Do you understand the importance of what was just covered? If you need to, stop and go back and reread it and emblazon these truths in your head.

It's Time to Stand Up for the Truth
Dietrich Bonhoeffer, a Christian pastor in Germany who was martyred for speaking up and exposing Hitler's lies, said the following, "Silence in the face of evil, is evil itself. God will not hold us guiltless. Not to speak is to speak. Not to act is to act."

For decades I have challenged people to be bold and courageous as I've quoted this famous maxim: "All that is required for the triumph of evil is for good men to say nothing."

In an urgent hour when many atheists and "progressives" want to reshape America into a Godless nation contrary to our heritage, "the eyes of the Lord run to and fro throughout the whole earth in order to show Himself strong on behalf of those whose hearts are fully blameless towards Him" (2 Chron. 16:9).

Dr. Martin Luther King Jr. proclaimed the truth fearlessly. He gave his famous "I've Been to the Mountaintop" speech at the historic Mason Temple in Memphis, Tennessee, knowing intuitively that his stand for racial equality would cost him his life. The night before he was killed he told the people, "I've seen the promised land. I may not get there... But I want you to know tonight that we, as a people, will get to the promised land."

The next day he was killed. Dr. King helped secure historic victories in the fight for racial equality. The Civil Rights Act of 1964 banned discrimination in government, employment, and housing. The Voting Rights Act of 1965 followed. This bold servant of God made it possible.

When he was only 27 years of age and his life was being threatened, he cried out to God in desperation and, in his own words, here's what happened: "I could hear the quiet assurance of an inner voice, 'Martin Luther, stand up for righteousness. Stand up for justice. Stand up for truth. And lo, I will be with you even unto the end of the world.' I heard the voice of Jesus saying still to fight on. At that moment, I experienced the Presence of the Divine as I have never experienced Him before. Almost at once my fear began to go. My uncertainty disappeared. I was ready to face anything."

That same Presence and power will be with us as we compassionately and courageously stand up for truth in our generation. "The righteous are bold as a lion... " (Prov. 28:1).

During World War II, England's prime minister, Winston Churchill (one of my heroes), stood up strong when Hitler was steamrolling over Europe and even Churchill's own people were ready to capitulate to this demon-possessed dictator. This valiant leader rescued Western civilization through his stirring speeches. He invented the tank and aerial bombing and challenged his people with words like the following:

> *I expect that the Battle of Britain is about to begin. Upon this battle depends the survival of Christian civilization... If we can stand up to Hitler, all Europe may be free and the life of the world may move forward into broad sunlit uplands. But if we fail, then the whole world, including the United States, including all that we have known and cared for, will sink into the abyss of a new Dark Age... Let us therefore brace ourselves to our duties, and so bear ourselves that if the British Empire and its Commonwealth last for a thousand years, men will still say, "This was their finest hour!"*

As politicians, pundits, celebrities, musicians, and academic elites join forces with the so-called "progressives" and "New Atheists" to tear down the Judeo-Christian foundations of America, may we speak with courage and charity in what can be "our finest hour." We are all candidates to "hit the mark" and help others as we continue learning the issues and the answers from a biblical worldview.

Chapter 7
Happiness and Prosperity

What is the secret to happiness? How can a nation prosper?
Do you know who was the happiest person who ever lived? The answer is found in the Bible—it was Jesus!

Scripture tells us the following regarding Jesus Christ: "You love justice and hate evil. Therefore, oh God, your God has anointed you, pouring out the oil of joy on you more than on anyone else" (Heb.1:9 NLT).

Millions of people in our culture today reject not Jesus, but rather a caricature of Him. For countless millions of people, the person of Jesus Christ conjures up images of a poker–faced, wimpy, somewhat strange type of bearded killjoy who never smiled, always appeared somewhat emaciated, and had chubby little cherubs floating about his head along with a glowing frisbee! What a distortion of the true Son of God. My friend Mike Bickle says, "Most people think of Jesus as mainly sad and mainly mad but rarely glad!"

Unfortunately, many Christians are perceived the same way.

Now the reason Jesus was so joyful, happy, and free is that He followed the will of God the Father perfectly. This is sometimes called "Happy Holiness." In other words, living a life that is separate from self-centeredness and the counterfeit values of our culture will lead to actual happiness, peace, and joy, but it must be in that order.

The Coca-Cola corporation recently ran an ad with the headline "We Choose Happiness Over Tradition." The ad depicts two apparently gay guys with their "adopted" baby and the above promotion for the homosexual lifestyle and same-sex marriage over traditional marriage between one man and one woman in covenant commitment.

Discerning Christians see the subtle pitch. We also know that living starts with holiness, not happiness, and pleasing God comes before personal pleasure. Through our Bullseye Challenge we hope to develop our level of discernment so we're more perceptive of the propaganda in our culture while being able to answer charitably and clearly on the hot-button issues of our day.

Democrat, Republican, Independent, Libertarian, Liberal, Conservative, or a Discerning Person?

In an era of increasing deception, from computer–enhanced cover girls, phony photos and backgrounds on dating sites, plus "reality shows" that aren't real after all, we have to be vigilant. In the New Testament, Jesus warned us that at the end of the age prior to His return, the number one signpost would be "deception." He says it three times in Matthew 24:1-10.

Ideas in our culture are swirling around with no consequences when they are embraced. *Ideas have consequences.* Why don't you pause and look at that three-word sentence again and let it be seared into your brain?

In 1964, an epic three–hour film was released called *The Rise and Fall of the Roman Empire.* The opening line of this film was the following: "The two biggest questions in history are: 1. How Rome rose? 2. How Rome fell? This is the story. It was not an event but a process. It did not happen overnight."

Rome wasn't built in a day, but its collapse didn't happen in a day either. Evil that brings destruction follows a pattern. First comes Accommodation, then Acceptance, and finally Adoption. Survey the scene today in our nation and you'll see how we've witnessed this with abortion, cohabitation, drug usage, gay marriage, etc., etc. As we cited in yesterday's lesson, there are people committed to dismantling our Judeo-Christian foundations in reshaping America as a secular society. "Tear it down," they cried. "Tear it down to its foundations!" (Ps. 137:7).

Understanding these realities, and desiring to be an informed influencer and agent of change in my generation, I ask myself, "should I identify as a Republican, Democrat, Independent, Moderate, Libertarian, Liberal, Conservative, Left–wing, or Right-wing, or how about the whole bird?! Do I even understand what these labels and party affiliations stand for today?"

Here's the deal: you can call yourself whatever you want, just as long as you know what that identification stands for and you always remain a discerning person on your journey. Consider the wisdom spoken by Peter Marshall, former Chaplain of the U.S. Senate: "Give us clear vision that we may know where to stand and what to stand for— because unless we stand for something, we shall fall for anything."

A Crash Course in Civics, Since We Don't Get it in School Anymore! Political parties are our American way of accomplishing things by coalescing people around particular agendas. United action increases effectiveness. Let an ox pull a cart and he can pull 1000 pounds. Yoke two oxen together and they can pull 5000 pounds. It's amazing but true.

As a boy, I asked my parents what the difference was between a Democrat and a Republican. Being poor (my dad never finished high school and was a maintenance man, and my mom a cleaning lady, plus we never had a car or went on vacations) and not that well educated, they gave me this response: "Democrats care about hard-working folks. Republicans are a bunch of big shots and fat cats who are rich." Not too fair and balanced, right?

Many black Americans gravitate to the Democratic Party today based on similar input. Historically it was Abraham Lincoln, a member of the Republican Party, who led the way to abolish slavery. Let's remind ourselves also that Republican Martin Luther King Jr.'s historic speech on the Mall was focused in large part at persuading a resistant Democratic Congress to finally act on civil rights legislation! When Presidents John F. Kennedy and Lyndon Johnson seized the initiative to advance civil rights in the 1960s, the tide basically turned. Today Republicans are working to reverse this trend and also reach Hispanics, who are now the largest minority in America.

What is critical for us is to keep something in mind. When you back a candidate, it should not be because he or she is charismatic, or "cool" or represents a "first" or a particular label. We must learn to ask difficult and revealing questions such as, "What do they stand for?" and "What is their party's platform?" and "What kind of a person are they?"

In the Bible, God gave criteria for a civil magistrate in Deuteronomy 1:4–18 and Exodus 18:21. It was important that individuals were wise, respected, fair, capable, trustworthy, honest, and feared God. Notice the importance of character before charisma?

To help us remember these criteria, here is an acrostic: C. H. E. A. P. In other words, don't skimp when it comes to the following:

- Character: good, bad or suspect?
- History: Where did they come from? What's their background?
- Experience: What has it been, and for how long?
- Accomplishments: What have they achieved, and what's the fruit?
- Platform: What issues do they support and oppose?

What's the Basic Difference Between a Liberal and a Conservative?
Conservative: One who wants to conserve/hold on to what's "right."

Liberal: One who wants to liberalize/free society from what's "wrong."

Both have merit, yet both can go wrong.

Example: When someone in the past wanted to "conserve" the *status quo*, such as women not voting, blacks not considered equal, and voting rights being restricted, this was not good.

Example: Individuals want to "liberate" society from moral standards and its heritage to reshape America into countries with Europe's socialism and Amsterdam's liberalism. This definitely is not good.

It is so important that we recover what our Founding Fathers intended and what our nation embraced for three-and-a-half centuries prior to the 1960s upheaval we discussed. While Jesus is not sitting in heaven waving an American flag and humming "God Bless the USA," let's remember that the United States of America has been an example for centuries to the rest of the world. The vision of the

Christians who established this nation was as a "city on the hill," bringing the gospel and being a witness to the world.

One of our greatest presidents, Ronald Reagan, also cited this reference that came from the Sermon on the Mount when he spoke to Americans in a time of great turmoil. He inspired hope and led us into a tremendous time of recovery and prosperity during which he stood firm against communism and eventually we saw the collapse of the Soviet Union and the Berlin Wall! In 1964 he said these words:

> *"You and I have a rendezvous with destiny. We will preserve for our children this, the last best hope of man on earth, or we will sentence them to take the last step into a thousand years of darkness."*

Previously, Americans enjoyed the blessings of balance between the political parties that was derived from the moral consensus based on a biblical worldview. As people drifted from this orientation, many are now adrift on the sea of moral uncertainty. Over eight percent of Americans agree that we are off-track. So the question before us is "Do we try to further liberate our country from its moorings or do we conserve and reclaim our foundations?"

Contrary to what many put forth as the "inherent goodness of man," the Bible and our forefathers recognized the inherent sinfulness of man. Therefore they established checks and balances on power. This is why we have three branches of government: the executive, the legislative and the judicial. Some politicians try to maneuver around these safeguards and act in more autocratic, independent ways. This is arrogance and is very detrimental to our future. "Power corrupts and absolute power corrupts absolutely."

Our Declaration of Independence was based on Judeo-Christian principles, not guesswork. Secularists want to avoid this reality and distort this through falsehoods and manipulation of the historical facts. This founding document mentions God four times, describing Him as:

- "Our Creator"
- "Nature's God"

- "Supreme Judge of the World"

- "Our Divine Protector, on whom we rely"

It asserted that all of us are endowed by our Creator with certain God-given rights—life, liberty and the pursuit of happiness. "Life" includes the right to life (from conception until natural death). "Liberty" does not mean freedom to do whatever one wants, but responsibility to do as one ought (Divine and civil laws restrict immoral and illegal behavior to balance order and freedom. For example, people can't yell "Fire!" in a crowded theater or carry guns on planes or run naked through a school). "Pursuit of happiness" includes the privilege to seek a prosperous, fulfilling life as a result of one's honest labors. "Happiness" did not mean drunkenness, revelry, or unrestrained promiscuity, but the term actually refers to a virtuous life with its rewards.

Another one of our Founding Fathers, Samuel Adams (that's not the beer, but the man!), stated these sobering words:

> *The liberties of our country and the freedom of our civil Constitution are worth defending against all hazards; it is our duty to defend them against all attacks. We have received them as a fair inheritance from our worthy ancestors. They purchased them for us with toil and danger and expense of treasure and blood and transmitted them to us with care and diligence. It will bring an everlasting mark of infamy on the present generation, enlightened as is, if we should suffer them to be wrestled from us by violence without a struggle, or to be cheated out of them by the artifices of false and designing men.*

Responding to those who would deny our religious roots and attempt to hijack our heritage, let's conclude by letting our history speak for itself. May you decide to pursue happiness the way Jesus Christ modeled and our forefathers envisioned. May you also be discerning and communicate to others the truth of America's heritage and why we have been the most blessed nation on the face of the earth.

It didn't come by coincidence, but Providence. It also can be lost in a generation if we don't guard the sacred trust.

Our True History

- The Mayflower Compact stated the reasons the Pilgrims came to America: "For the glory of God and advancement of the Christian faith…"

- The constitutions of all of the original 13 colonies acknowledged God and mandated scriptural education in the public schools. The one textbook used by nearly every public school student was the McGuffey Reader, which said, "The Scriptures are specially designed to make us wise unto salvation through faith in Jesus Christ."

- Our first Congress began with a three-hour prayer meeting and Bible study.

- George Washington took his oath of office with his hand on an open Bible and he added his own words, "So help me God," now repeated by every president since.

- Bibles were printed at taxpayers' expense and distributed widely while Christian chaplains were appointed in the Congress and US military.

- Our oldest colleges were Christ-centered, Bible-based, and mainly established for training individuals for ministry and proclamation of the Gospel.

- The US Supreme Court building served as a church every Sunday until the 1850s and, during President Thomas Jefferson's two terms, the largest church in America met every Sunday in the US Capitol building.

- When the Constitutional convention was deadlocked in 1787, Ben Franklin called the assembly to prayer, quoting the Bible: "Unless the Lord builds the house, the laborers work in vain" (Ps. 127:1). After a recess they gathered back together and drew up the document that Gladstone called "the most wonderful

work ever struck off at a given time by the brain and
purpose of man."

The Faith Factor of Our Founding Fathers
"Blessed is the nation whose God is the Lord" (Ps. 33:12).
Let's conclude today's segment by listening once again to some
of our early patriots, regardless of their party affiliation, yet united
in their convictions and faith:

*"It cannot be emphasized too strongly or too often that
this great nation was founded not by religionists, but by
Christians, not on other religions but on the gospel of
Jesus Christ."*
—Patrick Henry

*"The highest glory of the American Revolution was this:
it connected in one indissoluble bond the principles of
civil government with the principles of Christianity"*
—President John Q. Adams

*"Do not let anyone claim the tribute of American patri-
otism if they attempt to remove religion from politics. If
they do that, they cannot be true Americans,"*
—President George Washington

*"We have no government armed with power capable of
contending with human passions unbridled by morality and religion. Our Constitution was made only for a
moral and religious people. It is wholly inadequate to
the government of any other."*
—President John Adams

*"Can the liberties of a nation be thought secure when
we have removed their only firm basis, a conviction in
the minds of the people that these liberties are the gift of
God? That they are not to be violated but with his wrath?
Indeed I tremble for my country when I reflect that God
is just and that His justice cannot sleep forever"*
—President Thomas Jefferson

"I've lived a long time, and the longer I live, the more convincing proofs I see of this truth: that God governs in the affairs of men. If a sparrow cannot fall to the ground without His notice, is it probable that an empire can rise without His aid? We've been assured in the sacred writings that 'unless the Lord builds the house, they labor in vain who build it.' I firmly believe this, and I also believe that without His concurring aid, we shall succeed in this political building no better than the builders of Babel"
                                                    —Benjamin Franklin

"The Bible is the best of all books, for it is the Word of God and teaches us the way to be happy in this world and in the next. Continue therefore to read it and to regulate your life by its precepts...Providence has given to our people the choice of their rulers, and it is the duty, as well as the privilege and interest of our Christian nation, to select and prefer Christians for their rulers."
                                —First Chief Justice of the Supreme Court, John Jay

And now one final quotation, from a visitor to America who came to learn the secret of our prosperity and well-being as a nation. Alexis de Tocqueville was a French observer who came in 1831 and later wrote "Democracy in America" from his observations. In it, he said:

"There is no country in the world where the Christian religion retains a greater influence over the souls of men than in America... America is great because America is good. If she ever ceases to be good, she will cease to be great."

Chapter 8
Evaluating Politicians

Case Study: Barack Obama

> *"But examine everything carefully; hold fast to that which is good; abstain from every form of evil."*
>
> —I Thess. 5:21-22

Moving forward with our Bullseye Challenge, let's pause and put into practice some things we've learned about discernment, devotion to Biblical truth, and avoiding deception. Let's examine a political figure in a respectful yet Biblical way. As I did at the outset with Ellen DeGeneres, now let me attempt to model an imaginary interaction with Barack Obama even after he's vacated this high office. Maintaining a right spirit and speaking in a humble manner (but not shrinking back from core issues), I invite you to accompany me into the conversation:

Sir, I thank you for this opportunity to speak with you to help those taking our Bullseye Challenge. Let me begin with a little something about myself.

After graduating from Cleveland State University, where I was privileged to serve as the president of our student body, I was selected for a post at the AFL-CIO headquarters across the street from the White House. One day I bumped into President Nixon as he exited his limo, and I asked him this question: "Mr. President, do you read the Bible?"

The smile he tried to swallow surfaced on his face as he replied with a wink and a nod. "I not only read it; I even quote from it sometimes!"

Although Richard Nixon knew Bible verses, when I reflect on that interchange I still wonder if he was really a born-again Christian. The fruit and witness of his life are a tragedy and make it suspect, so I leave the eternal destiny of this departed leader in the hands of God.

Mr. Obama, would you allow me to share with you that I and scores of others have similar doubts about your conversion and the authenticity of your Christianity? I say up front that while I'm in disagreement with many of your policies and beliefs, I do love you and pray for you every single day. I affirm your God-given gift of leadership and your exemplary role as a husband and a father to your two lovely daughters. Yet I must be honest with you: I'm not sure you're really a Christian.

Will you allow me to present my reasons and, if you're not, to challenge you to become a true disciple of Jesus Christ at a time when America desperately needs moral leadership whether as president or beyond this office? After political leader William Wilberforce was genuinely converted, he became the leader in the abolition of the slave trade in England that reverberated later to America. He brought about a righteous transformation, but it was accomplished after a true born-again experience that catapulted him to victory because of the blessing of God on his life.

Former President George W. Bush exemplary in his attitude toward you since leaving the White House, and maybe this statement gives us a clue into his similar experience. He said, "When you turn your heart and your life over to Christ, when you accept Christ as the Savior, it changes your heart." This he learned after a soul-searching conversation with Billy Graham that led him to his born-again experience.

A changed life is at the core of a genuine conversion experience. This is what separates the authentic from the counterfeit when so many Americans—some polls say eighty percent—profess to be Christian, yet something seems terribly amiss as we survey our society today. And with all due respect, that's where I and countless others find ourselves sincerely questioning your stated spiritual identity of "I'm a Christian."

Are you?

Not that long ago, another former president, Jimmy Carter, shared that his conversion to Christ came when confronted by this challenging inquiry: "If you were arrested for being a Christian today, would there be enough evidence to convict you?" Convicted of his religious hypocrisy and self-righteousness, the peanut farmer from Plains, Georgia, repented and was genuinely born again, as Jesus stated each person must be in order to become a child of God. Admittedly, where he's at today is another story!

Immediately this poses a problem with your expressed theology. Scripture clearly teaches that while all people are loved by God, are created in God's image, and are to be treated with dignity as God's creation, only those who repent and put their total trust in God's only begotten Son are designated children of God (see John 1:12). That may not be popular or politically correct, but it's fact according to divine revelation.

Yet you say what scores of people mistakenly or ignorantly embrace: "I believe that there are many paths to the same place, and that is a belief that there is a higher power, a belief that we are connected as a people. We are all children of God."

Being incorrect on this fundamental of the faith is but one of many areas that cause many to sincerely question your understanding of the true nature of Christianity, as well as the legitimacy of your conversion. And if you hold that we all are God's children, why won't you defend the least of these and most vulnerable—the unborn? Your one hundred percent NARAL pro-abortion rating, your endorsement of taxpayer dollars for Plan B contraception, your support of partial-birth abortion, your opposition to the Born-Alive Infants Protection Act and your speech to Planned Parenthood that ended with "God bless you!" leaves us dumbfounded.

Before leaving office you gave a speech to the Catholic Health Association of the United States and related how your first job after college made you realize that "every human being, made in the image of God, deserves to live in dignity." You also stated, "All children... ought to have the opportunity to achieve their God-given potential."

Sir, one of the issues we'll tackle in our thirty-day experience is social justice and protection of human life—the unborn, the poor, the disabled, the mentally challenged, the elderly, and AIDS victims. With all due respect, how can you reconcile your unfettered support for abortion with your "Christian" faith?

Lest you and others stiffen at this point and say, "Hold it! Religion is personal. That's disrespectful. Doesn't the Bible state, 'Judge not'?" Let's be clear here on what Jesus actually said. He stated, "Judge with righteous judgment" (John 7:24) while cautioning us to avoid anything hypocritical, mean-spirited, or un-redemptive.

When it comes to leaders, righteous judgment is not an elective but a directive, so we'll know their character and the values that shape their positions on critical issues affecting our lives. Also, we must examine their fruit (what they're producing), which takes time, something I and millions have afforded you. To simply give you a pass here because of the historic nature of your election or because of your race is idolatry and must be categorically rejected once and for all. America is imploding rapidly, and we cannot afford to remain ignorant or complacent, or to retreat at this watershed moment.

Jesus Christ stated, "Every good tree bears good fruit, but a bad tree bears bad fruit" (Matt. 7:17). While I honored you in your position, I humbly submit that we've seen lots of "bad fruit" coming from a tree most likely in need of real redemption. The Good News of the gospel begins with this recognition!

Examining your beliefs, policies, social leanings, and character lead us to this reasonable conclusion. Many of them are inconsistent with living out the Biblical worldview that is to characterize an authentic, obedient Christian. It also encourages other high-profile Catholic Christians like Nancy Pelosi and Caroline Kennedy to continue in their wayward paths.

We all know you went to a Catholic school in a Muslim country. I, too, had twelve years of parochial school upbringing but wasn't truly born again until the age of twenty. Later, after an admitted lifestyle of drug use and fornication (cohabitation), you straightened out somewhat in Chicago and joined Trinity United Church of Christ, pastored by Jeremiah Wright.

You spent twenty years there but later disassociated yourself as public scrutiny of the Reverend and his teachings became uncomfortable for you. As I proceed, know that I definitely cut you some slack here because this represents your formative years in the Christian faith. We know that the content of a church's message determines the authenticity of its converts.

My question to you is this: Have you ever received correct instruction in the Christian faith? It's probably uncomfortable to hear this forthright and honest inquiry into your spiritual life, but we all need people in our lives who will tell us not what we want to hear, but what we need to hear. What is at stake is your eternal destiny.

Franklin Graham was asked not long ago about your faith. He's an honest man who pulls no punches. "I don't know if he's a Christian," he said.

On the other hand, your former religious adviser, Joshua DuBois, appeared on national TV once promoting his book, *The President's Devotional.* He testified to your faith in glowing terms, saying you're "a committed Christian. ... He practices his faith, spending time in the Oval Office with pastors praying for him. ... He went up the side of a mountain to visit Billy Graham. ... He has a yearly prayer call with pastors on his birthday. ... He really lives it out. ... I'd rather have a leader who lives a sermon than preaches one!"

These are all commendable activities, but most of us know atheists, Buddhists, Muslims, Hindus, and humanitarians who also are good husbands and fathers, who pray with others, who do good deeds and visit the sick. What really matters is this: Are they—and are you—born again?

Jesus told a learned, very religious man, "Unless one is born again, he cannot see [or enter] the kingdom of God" (John 3:3, 5). How's that for straight talk?

Years ago, Charles Colson, White House special counsel and "hatchet man" for President Nixon, was radically transformed when he repented and yielded his life to Jesus Christ. He penned a bestseller entitled *Born Again* to share his journey. May I suggest it for your next reading? Jesus said, "Not everyone who says to Me, 'Lord, Lord,' shall enter the kingdom of heaven, but he who does the will of My Father in heaven" (Matt. 7:21). The key here is not merely a declaration but a demonstration—obedience to God's Son and His Words as revealed in sacred Scripture.

Years ago, at Moody Church in your hometown of Chicago, a famous pastor spoke with an elderly man who confessed to the pastor his uncertainty about his conversion experience. He told the pastor how he longed for some definite witness that he could not mistake.

"Suppose," said the pastor, "that you had a vision of an angel who told you your sins were forgiven and you were genuinely converted. Would that be enough to rest on?"

"Yes," the man replied. "I think it would. An angel would be great!"

The pastor continued. "Suppose that on your deathbed Satan came and said, 'I was that angel, transformed to deceive you.' What would you say then?"

The gentleman was speechless.

The pastor smiled and put his arm around the shoulder of the older gentleman and said the following: "God has given us something much more trustworthy and authoritative than the voice of an angel. Consider that an angel supposedly launched the Mormon faith and Islam! God has given us His Son and His authoritative Word."

That is enough to rest on—if we will humble ourselves and follow in obedience.

The Seven Biblical Marks of an Authentic Christian
Mr. Obama, the words of the Lord Jesus Christ are clear about what it really means to be His disciple, a Christian. There is scarcely any room for misunderstanding if we will accept what He says at face value. Here are the terms as communicated by the Savior Himself:

1. A supreme love for Jesus Christ (Luke 14:26)

2. A denial of self (Matt. 16:24)

3. A deliberate choosing of the cross (Matt. 16:24)

4. A life spent following Christ (Matt. 16:24)

5. A fervent love for all who belong to Christ (John 13:35)

6. An unswerving continuance in His Word (John 8:31)

7. A forsaking of all to follow Him (Luke 14:33).

I must alert you, as Jesus did those to whom He preached, that it is wise to first "count the cost." There are many positions you hold that are totally incompatible with Biblical teaching, no matter how many liberal Bible scholars have told you otherwise. These positions will have to change if you follow Jesus and obey His Word.

For instance:

- "Jesus is a historical figure for me, and he's also a bridge between God and man ... and he's also a wonderful teacher." *Jesus Christ is fully God and fully man.*

- "I believe there are many paths to the same place, and that is a belief that there is a higher power." *There is salvation in no one else except through Jesus Christ, God's only begotten Son.*

- "I'm a big believer in tolerance. I'm a progressive Christian." *While we should respect everyone's beliefs, we can't respect everyone's conduct.*

- "I find it hard to believe that my God would consign four-fifths of the world to hell." *The path to salvation is open to all, but it is narrow, excluding all who reject God's free gift of eternal life in Jesus Christ.*

- "Parts of the Bible may be modified to accommodate modern life." *Extreme caution is needed here, as we have a mandate to "rightly divide the Word of truth" (2 Tim. 2:15).*

- "What I believe in is that if I live my life as well as I can, I will be rewarded. I don't presume to have knowledge of what happens after I die." • •*Salvation comes as a result not of good deeds we do, but totally as a gift of God received by faith and with a certainty of heaven upon one's death. (Eph. 2:8-9).*

- "Those opposed to abortion cannot simply invoke God's will—they have to explain why abortion violates some principle that is accessible to people of all faiths." *At conception, a separate human being is created in God's image and deserves full protection and care until the child is born.*

- Regarding homosexuality and gay marriage, "I am not willing to accept a reading of the Bible that consists of an obscure line from Romans to be more defining of Christianity than the Sermon on the Mount." *Throughout the entire Bible, the practice of homosexuality is declared as sinful and contradictory to God's design for human relationships, marriage, and family.*

Thank you for listening, Mr. Obama! If what I have communicated resonates with you, I'd suggest you give a call to the Reverence Billy Graham, or is son, Franklin. Let him pray with you, as he has other presidents and former presidents for decades. What a phenomenal gift it would be to this true Christian statesman who has spent his lifetime introducing people to an authentic relationship with God's only begotten Son, Jesus Christ. And when Dr. Graham passes away, please talk with his son.

Respectfully, I am
Larry Tomczak

Chapter 9
Islam

Have We Been Told The Truth About Islam?
In the 1970s, Graham Nash of Crosby, Stills, Nash, and Young wrote a song called "Teach Your Children Well." It emphasized the societal impact of messages given to children. The smooth-as-silk melody continues to receive airplay. Recall the words?

"You who are on the road must have a code that you can live by, and so become yourself because the past is just a goodbye. Teach your children well... Just look at them and sigh and know they love you."

Political leaders, educators, and journalists should heed the point of teaching not only children well but also the general populace. Unfortunately, when it comes to the topic of Islam, many have communicated misinformation when they should have told the truth. During his time in office, Barack Obama did us a great disservice by distorting Islam's role in America's history as well as by disseminating falsehoods on this political ideology/religious system. Truth be known, he was both inaccurate and dishonest in what he communicated to Americans and others overseas:

- "Islam has been woven into the fabric of our country since its founding" (2015).

- "Islam has always been part of America" (2010).

- "I also know that Islam has always been a part of our American story" (2009).

- "This holiday (the Muslim holiday of Eid) reminds us of the many achievements and contributions of Muslim Americans to building the very fabric of our nation and strengthening the core of our democracy" (2014).

The impression created was one of Muslims being instrumental in establishing the United States of America right from its inception. The narrative highlights their supposed accomplishments and contributions in making our great nation what it is today.

It sounds sentimental and politically correct, but it wasn't true no matter how many times it was reiterated and affirmed by uninformed, planted people nodding their affirmation as they stood behind Obama as he spoke.

At the outset, let me say that as a true Christian, I love every person no matter what, and am passionate about sharing the gospel with everyone. A wonderful experience my wife and I shared a while ago was opening our home repeatedly to a Muslim couple for meals and conversation and then seeing them come to Christ and be baptized weeks later. It's critical to believe that there are "moderate" Muslims who are reachable as we engage them with the love and truth of mankind's only Lord and Savior, Jesus Christ!

It's also important to recognize that it is not just a miniscule minority of Muslims who support jihad and global domination. Pew Research revealed that twenty-two percent of the Muslim population are in this camp—more than the entire population of the United States of America! Islamic ideology is frightening and forthright in its core tenets.

Moment of Truth: Expose the Myths
President John F. Kennedy said the following in the 1960s: *"The great enemy of the truth is very often not the lie—deliberate, contrived or dishonest, but the myth—persistent, persuasive and unrealistic. Belief in myths allows the comfort of opinion, without the discomfort of thought."*

Communist revolutionary Vladimir Lenin said, *"If you can separate people from their history, they are easily persuaded."*

English author Samuel Johnson said *"People need to be reminded more than they need to be instructed."*

So let's not be separated from our history by reminding ourselves of our nation's founding and dispel any myths, even if they came from a president of the United States. And remember that Barack Hussein Obama was shaped by Islam: his father was a Muslim, he was given a Muslim name, his mother married another Muslim after her divorce from his father, and he was educated in Indonesia by Muslims.

Criticism in a right spirit is not unpatriotic. One of the greatest leaders of all time, Winston Churchill, told us, *"Criticism may not be agreeable, but it is necessary. It fulfills the same function as pain in the body. It calls attention to an unhealthy state of things."*

Wasn't it interesting that after Israeli Prime Minister Benjamin Netanyahu spoke the truth to Congress not long ago about Iran and its nuclear capabilities, he was presented with a bust of Winston Churchill? Contrast this with President Obama who, upon his election, returned to England the bust of Winston Churchill that had been given to President George W. Bush!

"Just the Facts, Ma'am"

Sgt. Joe Friday on the classic police drama *Dragnet* always insisted, "Just the facts." So what are the facts on America's founding and any Muslim role in it? What is the nature of Islam itself?

- No Muslims were signers of the Declaration of Independence. All but two or three of the fifty-six signers of the Declaration and Constitution were Bible-believing Christians. Many were ministers and those who weren't (like Ben Franklin) shared a basic Biblical worldview.

- The Quran had no place or even mention in the founding of the United States. Our founders had a Christian view of law—God and the Scriptures were the source of law for our nation.

- The Mayflower Compact stated the reason why the Pilgrims came to America: "For the glory of God and the advancement of the Christian faith." There is absolutely no mention of Islam in any of our founding documents!

- The constitutions of all of the original 13 colonies acknowledged Jesus Christ and mandated scriptural education in the public schools. The one textbook used by nearly every public school student was the McGuffey Reader, which said, *"The Scriptures are especially designed to make us wise unto salvation through faith in Jesus Christ."* There is no mention of Mohammed or Allah or the Muslim faith.

- George Washington took his oath of office with his hand on an open Bible and he added his own words, "So help me God" (not Allah), which have been repeated by every president since.

- Christian chaplains were appointed in the Congress and military and Bibles were printed at taxpayers' expense.

- The US Supreme Court building served as a church every Sunday until the 1850s and during President Thomas Jefferson's two terms, the largest church in America met every Sunday in the U.S. Capitol building. It is interesting to note that the Muslims' first mosque in America was built in North Dakota in 1929!

- John Jay, the first chief justice of the US Supreme Court, declared, *"The Bible [not the Quran] is the best of all books, for it is the Word of God and teaches us the way to be happy in this world and in the next. Continue therefore to read it and to regulate your life by its precepts ... Providence has given to our people the choice of their rulers, and it is the duty, as well as the privilege and interest of our Christian nation, to select and prefer Christians for their rulers."*

- Beginning with the establishment of our nation in 1620 by the Pilgrims at Plymouth Rock and spanning 250 years, can you find even a handful of prominent Muslim innovators or achievements of significance? You will find thousands of innovations, achievements, and innovations from the patriots of our country—those who were Judeo-Christian adherents. This is the true fabric of America, not some trumped-up fantasy figures!

• As the United States of America was being founded, Muslims were primarily slave traders in Africa, enslaving blacks, kidnapping them, and sending them here via the Dutch.

• Upon in-depth research, one can discover that in 1732 there is mention of a Muslim slave sent back to England by James Oglethorpe of Georgia; in 1807 there is reference to a Muslim who bought some shares in a bank; in 1828 there is mention of a Muslim in jail visited by John Owen, who later became governor of South Carolina; and, in 1856 during the Western advance, Jefferson Davis, then Secretary of War, hired a Muslim to help in raising camels who were well-suited for extended battles on the plain.

• During the early decades of America's founding, our leaders faced four decades of Muslim terrorism. In modern-day Morocco, Algeria, Libya, and Tunisia, Muslims kidnapped American sailors, looted American ships and captured Americans to sell them as slaves. The Heritage Foundation states that *"During America's founding it was dragged into the affairs of the Islamic world by an escalating series of unprovoked attacks on America by Muslim pirates, the terrorists of the era."*

Finally, in 1804, President Thomas Jefferson ordered the US Navy and Marines into Tripoli to stop the terrorism of Islamists. The military engagement marked the first time that a U.S. flag was raised on foreign soil and the first time that US power was projected abroad. To this day the United States Marine anthem begins with, "From the halls of Montezuma to the shores of Tripoli." The very nickname for Marines as "Leathernecks" came from the leather neck-piece that was part of their uniform to protect them from beheadings (sound familiar?).

- President Jefferson was a brilliant academic and did something that we would do well to imitate. He secured a copy of the Quran from England and studied its tenets. He then called Muhammad a "military fanatic" and one who "denies that laws were made for him; he arrogates everything to himself by force of arms."

- Finally, as Mr. Obama once lectured the Christians at the National Prayer Breakfast concerning the Crusades (Christian leader Star Parker labeled it "verbal rape"), facts from history tell us that in the 800s Muslims were taking control of the entire Mediterranean territory. It was not until 250 years later that the first Crusade was initiated to stop Muslim aggression, advancement, and destruction of human lives. My friend Nicholas Papanicolaou, author of *Islam vs. the United States*, says it best: "We must immediately change the narrative that our president is presenting and stop indicting Christians falsely for their response to terrorism and destruction by Muslims during the era of the Crusades."

- Exactly 100 years ago Armenian Christians were being slaughtered by Islamic militants during a seven-year period. The parallels to ISIS and their savage aggression today are frighteningly similar. One major difference: America did not remain silent or retreat. We were the Armenians' biggest defender! Pastors across this nation informed their congregations, and financial aid, along with prayers and volunteers, helped bring about rescue and recovery.

Today the drumbeat gets louder each day with militant jihadis drawing their ideology from the Quran and their perceived lack of morality in the West—pornography, fornication, adultery, cohabitation, homosexuality, and casual divorce. Many of ISIS's young men are recruited as they serve to cleanse themselves of guilt for earlier viewing of pornography coming from us.

While it may be unpleasant for some to admit, Islam has a long-standing historical record as a violent political ideology bent on world domination, masquerading as a "religion of peace." In spite of centuries of historical facts to the contrary and the violence promoted throughout Muslim writings themselves, some politicians and pundits continue to state publically that Islam is a religion of peace and that Muslim terrorists and militants don't represent the true nature of Islam.

This is just not the truth! Let me quote from a booklet that is available from the Christian Broadcasting Network entitled "Islam—Religion of Peace or War?"

"Their brutality knows no bounds. Since the beginning of the Islamic conquest until now, those slain by Muslim forces are as follows: Over fifty-one million Christians (many place the number at sixty million) were slaughtered. Eighty million Hindus were killed in jihad against ancient India. Jihadists killed ten million Buddhists in Turkey, Afghanistan, along the Silk Route, and in India. And upwards of 125 million Africans were slain, as Islam ran the wholesale slave trade in Africa..."

We need to wake up and see what is happening to Christians being slaughtered today in various parts of the world. After all our generals advised President Obama, when he was in office, to leave a strong "residual force" in Iraq he refused and pulled out with the disastrous consequences we are living with today. Imagine the genocide—once there were 1.5 million Christians there but now only 200,000 are left! The historical record proves that within four years after Mohammed's death and alleged ascension to heaven nearly 335,000 Christians were slaughtered and in ten years the number rose to one million!

As some politicians want to allow more illegal immigrants into this country, we must face the fact that we are also letting in individuals who have militant Islamic ties! While 466,000 illegal immigrants were captured, 157,000 got away unaccounted for! They came from 140 countries including Syria, Iran, and Iraq, and some are terrorists. It's naive to think that none are here! This is why we must secure the southern borders and recognize the realities of Islam, even though we know there are peaceful Muslims as well.

Here's the deal: We must start by understanding and facing the disturbing reality of this ideology and changing the narrative being rolled out by politicians today. It's not too late, but the clock is ticking. The challenge of Islam is a defining issue of our generation. May we teach our children well and awaken unaware multitudes.

> *"It cannot be emphasized too strongly or too often that this great nation was founded not by religioists, but by Christians, not on other religions but on the gospel of Jesus Christ."*
>
> —*Patrick Henry, American patriot*

Some individuals maintain that the Koran and Mohammed's life should both be viewed in two distinct parts—part one being the Islamic leader's initial attempt to spread his new religion more peacefully, yet with little success; and part two, which represents his violent, warrior approach that subjugated and slaughtered massed, reaping more territorial success. The latter is emulated by millions today because of their mission—a global caliphate with Muslims ruling the world. They are dead serious to accomplish this goal and mission.

Chapter 10
Solidarity Pledge

Three Pledges Every Christian Should Make in These Last Days

> *"When in the course of human events it becomes necessary for one people..."*

With these words, our Declaration of Independence begins.

The signers continued by affirming *"Nature's God,"* *"self-evident truths,"* and our *"Creator."* Then our brave forefathers, putting their very lives on the line, ended their statement of convictions by declaring, *"with a firm reliance on the protection of Divine Providence, we mutually pledge to each other our lives, our fortunes, and our sacred honor."*

At another historic moment, a courageous leader named Nehemiah led the people of God in a similar pledge that is recorded in the Bible (see Nehemiah 10:28-39). They promised to uphold marriage as God intended (verse 30) and *"obey carefully all the commands, regulations, and decrees of the Lord our God"* (verse 29).

Today the time has come, at a similarly defining moment, to follow these examples and collectively express our convictions so we will not waver in the difficult days ahead.

> *"Therefore, since we are encompassed with such a great cloud of witnesses, let us also lay aside every weight and the sin that so easily entangles us, and let us run with*

endurance the race that is set before us. Let us look to Jesus, the author and finisher of our faith" (Heb. 12:1-2a).

May we be found faithful as we draw upon His grace to be as He called us: "the salt of the earth" and the "light of the world."

Our Solidarity Pledge

1. We pledge to obey God, not government, regarding the sanctity of life and marriage.

Scripture tells us, *"Do not be conformed to this world, but be transformed by the renewing of your mind" (Rom. 12:2 NAS).* Therefore, any secular rulings contrary to God's will for unborn babies, marriage, and family cannot be honored by His obedient children. We will remain charitable but resolute that we will not capitulate.

The most innocent and defenseless in our midst must always be protected and given the right to life. And since the Bible begins and ends with marriage, we will remain faithful to uphold natural marriage between a man and a woman. The two legs upon which our society stands are these: the sanctity of life and the sanctity of marriage.

2. We pledge to honor our nation's scriptural, not secular, heritage.

Our Founding Fathers established our nation on Judeo-Christian foundations and pledged obedience to Him and divinely ordained standards. As a result, we have been blessed like no other nation in history.

Until recent generations, we basically remained faithful but now find ourselves seriously adrift from those principles that made America great. We pledge afresh to humbly endeavor to reclaim our godly heritage as "one nation under God, indivisible, with liberty and justice for all."

Founding Father Daniel Webster reminds us thusly:

If we and our posterity shall be true to the Christian religion, if we and they shall be always in the fear of God, and shall respect His commandments, if we and they shall maintain just moral sentiments and such conscientious convictions of duty as shall control the heart and life, we may have the highest hopes of the future fortunes of our

> *country . . . but if we and our posterity reject religious institutions and authority, violate the rules of eternal justice, trifle with the injunctions of morality, and recklessly destroy the political constitution which holds us together, no man can tell how sudden a catastrophe may overwhelm us, that shall bury all our glory in profound obscurity.*

3. We pledge to trust in God's protection amid judgment while praying for spiritual awakening.

The prophet Ezekiel was a "watchman on the wall" who warned people of impending judgment for continuing to violate God's righteous standards. Child sacrifice and disregarding divine standards for marriage and family brought discipline intended to turn people back to God.

For the remnant who remained faithful, God reassured them that amid severe punishment, righteous ones like Noah, Daniel, and Job were supernaturally protected (see Ezekiel 14:14). May we stand on their shoulders and experience similar deliverance.

In the meantime, we must resist the peril of familiarity and heed the promise of II Chronicles 7:14:

> *"If My people, who are called by My name, will humble themselves and pray, and seek My face and turn from their wicked ways, then I will hear from heaven, and will forgive their sin and will heal their land."*

Together we pledge to wholeheartedly turn away from any known sin in our own lives and return to wholehearted devotion to Jesus. We will remain courageous in boldly and charitably proclaiming God's Word. We also promise to give ourselves to evangelizing the lost as we believe in the possibility of Great Awakening such as those we have experienced twice in our nation's history.

Like our forefathers, we encourage each other and declare in unison:

> *"With a firm reliance on the protection of Divine Providence, we mutually pledge to each other our lives, our fortunes, and our sacred honor."*

We encourage you to post this pledge and pass it on for proclamation in public assemblies.

Chapter 11
Gay Marriage

What About Same-Sex Marriage?

What's the most weight a human ever lifted? Would you believe 6,270 pounds? In 1956 Olympic gold medalist (and Christian) Paul Anderson did this with a back lift.

I visited with his daughter years ago at his home and even though he's gone to heaven, his incredible record still stands.

What's the worst entrée in a national restaurant in America? Would you believe the Outback Steakhouse's Baby Back Ribs, containing over 3,000 calories and 242 grams of fat!?

Now what's the data on sexual-related issues revealing how "enlightened" or deceived we've become since the 1960s sexual revolution? Have we actually progressed or declined as a culture when we see the fruit?

1. *Divorce*: Increased from 4% to 51% since my child-hood; 46,523 weekly. The breakdown of the family is contributing to the breakdown of our nation. In the blockbuster movie *Jurassic World* a teenage boy consoles his younger brother, who is crying because their parents are divorcing, by saying "Hey, it's okay. All my friends' parents are divorced." This is a good thing? It's devastating. It's tragic.

2. *Cohabitation*: Sixty-five percent of "altar-bound" couples now live together (a euphemism for a lifestyle of fornication) before marriage. No commitment *before* conditions couples for little commitment *after*.

3. *Abortion/Infanticide/Euthanasia*: In forty years, we've killed over 58 million unborn babies (almost ten times the number of victims in Hitler's Holocaust), and now we do it with clever maneuverings using taxpayer funding and Obamacare. Two states have legalized "mercy killing" and deformed or unwanted babies are casually left to die in the culture of death that is emerging.

4. *Out-of-Wedlock Births*: For the first time in U.S. history it's more than fifty percent with resultant fatherless households and an orphaned generation. Increased crime, drugs, dropouts, and violence result as fathers are removed from families.

5. *Pornography*: Graphic sexual activity and nudity are now "just a click away" on computers and smartphones (generating more revenue than the NFL, the NBA, and MLB combined), destroying innocence while promoting deviancy.

6. *Homosexuality*: Lesbian, gay, bisexual, and transgender lifestyles are being endorsed and celebrated, along with same-sex marriage, school indoctrination, and new laws promoting this lifestyle, even though the percentage of gay Americans is only 1.7% (UCLA). Mainstream Christian denominations are compromising, and even granting the ordination of homosexuals.

7. *Sexually Transmitted Diseases*: According to the CDC (Centers for Disease Control), there are now over 110 million venereal diseases/infections amongst the American populace. This is now an epidemic.

A culture can spiral into sexual anarchy and lawlessness quickly when it removes God and His standards from its public life. Germany, an educated and civilized nation, moved from democracy to dictatorship and demise in less than six years! Can a once-thriving nation have its heritage and faith so decimated that history records it as a tragic collapse? The answer is *yes.*

In his final sermon, Billy Graham said, "I've wept for America." On his ninety-fifth birthday, he stated that the nation is "in great need of a spiritual awakening," something he prays for fervently every day.

Ronald Reagan once said, *"We can become one nation gone under instead of one nation under God."* He also stated that freedom is always *"one generation away from extinction"* if we don't courageously defend it. Retreat is not an option. Jesus said, "Occupy 'til I come." Obama's former Secret Service agent told us, "It's worse than people know...I'm not trying to scare you either."

As we continue our Bullseye Challenge, we cross over to the next category, "Sexuality, Marriage, and Relationships." The most controversial is "Same-Sex Marriage" so let's start here, pulling no punches. Buckle your seatbelt and remember that we will unfold this charitably yet clearly from a Scriptural worldview.

Ten Reasons Why Same-Sex Marriage is Wrong

> *"Don't tear down a fence until you know why it was put up."*
> —*African Proverb*

1. It violates the clear and unambiguous teaching of the Hebrew-Christian scriptures which serve as the basis for our Judeo-Christian laws and foundations as a nation. It distorts God's purpose for marriage as a picture of Christ's relationship with His Bride, the Church (Eph. 5:31-32).

2. It is contradictory to the self-evident truth of "Mother Nature" or "Nature's God" (as our Founding Fathers expressed it) wherein men and women are designed and function differently, complement and complete each other, and through the wonder of marital union are able to procreate with each other to perpetuate the cycle of life.

3. It is contrary to the explicit teaching of every major world religion which upholds the integrity of marriage and family.

4. It undermines the institution of marriage between a man and a woman that has been the cornerstone of civilization in custom and law for more than 5,000 years.

5. Not one civilized culture in the entire history of mankind (including those few that have been relatively tolerant of homosexuality) has ever sanctioned "marriage" between members of the same sex as a norm for family life.

6. It is an injustice and harmful arrangement wherein our most precious entrustment, our children, are denied the love and nurture of a father and a mother who complement each other in healthy family life, providing the optimum arrangement for health and success in life.

7. It redefines and devalues the sacred institution of marriage exclusively between a man and a woman, in addition to opening the door for other arrangements such as polygamy, polyamory, and pederasty (gay relationships between adult males and adolescent boys).

8. It is a radical social experiment like the disastrous "welfare state" and "no-fault divorce" ideas, which will further destabilize the already fragile family—the basic building block of our society.

9. It legitimizes, normalizes, and places an official stamp of approval on a lifestyle replete with dangerous, at-risk sexual behavior. This often leads to HIV/AIDS and over thirty STDs that endanger lives, jeopardize health care, and impact our economy.

10. It carries with it a plethora of new laws enacted to force compliance with the "progressive" agenda, while educating youth in what scripture labels "unnatural and shameful" sexual activity (Rom.1:18-27).

Chapter 12
Pornography, Profanity, and Immodesty

Bare the Truth?

Do standards exist anymore when it comes to pop culture and entertainment? Music festivals...movies...TV...How about dress? What do we do about porn and its availability?

Let's start with musical artistry on display at outdoor summer music fests like Bonnaroo (80,000 gather yearly about forty minutes from our house) or Lollapalooza (with 300,000 attendees each year).

What can go on at these events? Young people and parents, consider Chicago's Lollapalooza bash in Grant Park.

"C'mon you hot m---- f---ers! Give it up for the real Slim Shady ... EMINEM!!"

For the uninitiated, this Detroit rapper, part of the duo "Bad Meets Evil," has sold 115 million albums. He's a headliner. His life is a tale of debauchery, drugs, assault, arrest, divorce, and promotion of violence against women. His mother sued him. His best friend was shot in the head after killing someone. He's been addicted to drugs and alcohol, consuming forty to sixty Valium in a day. He overdosed on methadone—the equivalent of four bags of heroin. He was two hours from dying.

His songs are foul and profane, from the gutter. He peppers rhyming lyrics with the f-word and multitudes of obscenities while celebrating masturbation, violence, and references to a woman's intimate parts:

- "Kill You": "Slut, you think I won't choke no whore/ vocal cords don't work in her throat no more?"
- "We as Americans": "F--- money! I don't rap for dead presidents. I'd rather see the president dead."

"I can't hear ya, Chicago! Outkast is in the house! They've got that social stigma so let's make 'em feel right at home you (expletive) monsters!"

Again, for those not so clued in, these X-rated hip hop "artists" with attitude roll out a degree of depravity not comprehended by scores of adults. Sample some of the titles from their explicit album overflowing with profanities, *Speakerboxxx/The Love Below*:

- "Hootie Hoo"
- "She Lives in My Lap"
- "Toilet Tisha"
- "Gangsta Shxx"
- "2 Dope Boyz"
- "Where Are My Panties?"

Not every band sinks this low, but these were the headliners. Not everybody is in an inebriated stupor, but it's all around. There's nudity along with sex; twenty-one felony arrests (most drug-related); and the cleanup of 250 tons of trash, which includes drug paraphernalia, vomit, and unmentionables. And all this in an atmosphere where police usually turn a deaf ear and are encouraged not to be aggressive but let people "have a good time." The last time Lady Gaga performed, she launched her near-naked body to crowd-surf the riotous crowd.

Recently *Billboard* magazine ran an article entitled "17 Deaths and Counting: Festival Fatalities on the Rise." Even the music industry's bible is raising the red flag! Are parents paying attention? Even if there are no rapes, assaults, and felony gun charges cited, what are a parent's responsibilities in releasing a child or teenager into this kind of "free-for-all" environment of profanity, drugs, drunkenness, and sexually charged lyrics and examples?

How about shifting gears to check out films?

Recently my wife and I attended a decent movie, where we had an encounter with a Christian woman in the lobby. Making conversation, I inquired as to what film she was seeing and had to conceal my cringe when she told me the title of the flick.

"Are you aware of the content?" I gently inquired, as I had previously read a review. Not wanting to come across as self-righteous or critical, I bantered with her a bit about what she was about to partake of.

She giggled and then shrugged it off by saying, "Well, I already bought the ticket!"

At this, I smiled and said, "Nobody stands at entrances; there's a bunch of other decent flicks."

"Well...I like the actress who's one of the leads," she said.

I knew this was a losing cause.

What was it my sister in the Lord saw as she sat in that theater? An R-rated profane comedy starring "America's sweetheart" (from the godly film *The Blind Side*) featuring constant crude jokes about female and male genitals, 150 f-words, characters misusing God's name more than sixty times, adultery, violence (including people shot in the head and genitals, with blood spurting), drunkenness, cocaine use, stealing, and a nonstop barrage of human indecency.

"At least there weren't any major displays of nudity, homosexuality, or gore!" you might say.

True, but are Christians really in touch with what's happening today to entertainment? How many are rationalizing viewing pornography and are addicted to it? How many in our ranks are sadly being seduced to compromise and just "go with the flow"? We don't want to be accused of legalism, you know. And what about the area of appearance? How do we remain stylish and attractive, yet dress modestly and decently? Here's some help.

Navigating the Gray Areas
Religion can come up with lists of dos and don'ts, but those lists don't deal with our hearts. If we are determined to glorify God in every area of our life, may these ten questions help us

evaluate entertainment in order to walk in a manner pleasing to the Lord:

1. Is it beneficial—spiritually, mentally and physically— to me as a Christian? (1 Cor. 6:12)

2. Can I do it in fullness of faith? If I doubt, better do without! (Rom. 14:23)

3. Will it enslave me and bring me under its power? (1 Cor. 6:12)

4. Does it glorify God? (1 Cor. 10:31)

5. Is it good stewardship of time and/or money? (1 Cor. 4:2)

6. Will it dull my spirit and cause me to lose my edge in God? (Rom. 12:11)

7. Will it grieve (sadden) the Holy Spirit? (Eph. 4:30)

8. Will it edify others? Does it seek their good? (1 Cor. 10:33)

9. Is it worth imitating? (1 Cor. 11:1)

10. Could it cause others to stumble? (Rom. 14:21)

Normally evaluations are easy to make based on clear-cut Scripture teachings. Anyone justifying the viewing of pornography is deceived. Jesus told us not to ever "look lustfully upon a woman (Matt. 5:28) and Ps. 101:3 says, *"I will put no unclean thing before my eyes."* What follows are some guidelines to help us regarding decency and modesty in appearance.

Guidelines for Honoring God in Appearance
How we dress is addressed by God, so we can look attractive without inviting lustful looks which cause others to stumble. Most Christians are not deliberately dressing immodestly but rather drift into alluring clothes out of ignorance or a desire for acceptance. Modest attire starts in the heart, not the hemline, with a desire to honor God, *not* a dress code to inhibit man. May these guidelines help you in this time which has been called "the undressing of America":

1. We are to *"present our bodies to God as a living and holy sacrifice which is our reasonable worship and not be conformed to this world [pop culture] but be transformed by the renewing of our minds" (Rom. 12:1-2).* We should look sharp, not seductive. We can dress cool without appearing cheap. Let's draw attention to our countenance and eyes (which Jesus said are the "lamp of the body," as opposed to body parts and flesh that often show where a person's heart and focus really are). Let's not rationalize either ("I get a better tan line and guys shouldn't be looking anyway").

2. We know that we should never wear clothing that draws lustful looks, causing others to "stumble" into sin (Matt. 18:6) or commit adultery in their heart by fantasizing after viewing us dressed provocatively or immodestly (Matt. 5:28), i.e., wearing a swimsuit akin to walking around in revealing underwear. Let's get real: is some beach attire a "bathing suit" or almost a "birthday suit"? We must not allow ourselves to become desensitized to the message of modesty today.

3. Modesty is a positive principle emphasizing inner beauty and character over outward vanity and cheapness. *"I want women to dress with proper clothing, modestly and discreetly..."(1 Tim. 2:9).* "Sprayed on" leggings not covering well below the waist or "see-through," bra-less blouses don't get a thumbs up here. This applies equally to men! Sexy Speedos, skimpy bikinis, low-rise (underwear-showing) pants, low-rise (panty-showing) shorts and midriff-baring or "nice-and-tight" tee shirts should all be viewed through this lens:

   • Proper": suitable, appropriate, conforming to an acceptable standard, decent

   • "Modest": having a regard for decencies of behavior or dress, not displaying one's body.

   • "Discreet": lacking ostentation (showiness); showing good judgment

4. In the Garden of Eden, before sin entered into the world, the man and his wife were both naked (the Hebrew word speaks of partial covering, covered by God's glory) (Gen 2:25); after they sinned, the effect was shame, so they covered up (Gen.3:7)! *"The parts that are not presentable are treated with special modesty" (I Cor.12:23).* This is why we naturally feel self-conscious about body parts revealed; we fold arms under breasts, clasp hands in front of our lower anatomy when standing before a group, etc. God designed us in this way and we're most at peace when aligned with His plan. Pornography and provacative photo shoots entice onlookers but the participants are often on drugs, drinking (to lower inhibitions), or so desperate they'll act contrary to what they know deep down to be right. Stay away!

5. No matter how alluring and supposedly happy certain divas, models, and Hollywood superstars appear, don't be fooled. God tells us: *"Charm is deceitful and beauty is vain but the woman who fears the Lord, she shall be praised" (Prv 31:30).* Behind closed doors, many of these "picture-perfect" (and computer-enhanced, surgically altered) people are, in reality, lonely, jaded, and empty. They flit from romance to romance and therapist to therapist; "on the outside they appear beautiful but inside they are full of dead man's bones and all uncleanness" (Matt. 23:27). Pray for them!

6. We are "called to freedom but are not to use our freedom as an opportunity for the flesh [to indulge our sinful nature], rather serve one another in love" (Gal. 5:13). In other words, we have the privilege and the ability to defer to rather than defraud the opposite sex through sensuality. Again, here are the definitions:

   • "Defer": limiting my freedom in order not to offend those God allows me to serve (Rom. 14:21)

   • "Defraud": arousing sexual desires in another person that cannot be righteously satisfied (1 Thess. 4:6)

- "Sensuality": planned appeal to the physical senses for personal gratification (1 Pet. 2:11)

Let's ask: "Who dictates my wardrobe—worldly magazines, movies, and models or the Word of God, which calls me to be (as a woman): 1. Feminine 2. Modest 3. Appropriate and (as a man): 1. Masculine 2. Modest 3. Appropriate.

7. One of the clearest and most comprehensive passages in God's Word on the topic is 1 Thess. 4:2-6:

   For you know what instructions we gave you by the authority of the Lord Jesus. It is God's will that you should be sanctified: that you should avoid sexual immorality; that each of you should learn how to control his own body in a way that is holy and honorable, not in passionate lust like the heathen, who do not know God; and that in this matter no one should defraud his brother (or sister) or take advantage of him. The Lord will punish men for all such sins, as we have already told you and warned you.

8. When there is a question raised (by yourself, a parent, or a faithful friend) concerning an article of clothing, length of a skirt, level of a neckline, tightness of jeans, size of shorts, sheerness of a fabric, style of an outfit, or message on a shirt, follow the following:

   - Doubt—do without (Rom. 14:13)
   - "Flee youthful lusts" (2 Tim. 2:22)
   - "Honor your father and your mother" (Eph. 6:2-3).

9. Determine to be radical, biblical, and charitable in all you do. Don't give a flip what others think—only what God thinks! Be courageous. Have convictions. Live life to the hilt for God's glory!

   My son, if sinners entice you, do not give in to them...do not go along with them, do not set foot on their paths; for their feet rush into sin...But among you there must not be even a hint of sexual immorality, or of any kind

of impurity, or of greed, because these are improper for
God's holy people. (Prov. 1:10, 15-16; Eph. 5:3)

10. While taking time daily to look your best as a radiant Christian (guy or girl), make sure you spend equal or more time daily preparing your heart and mind by seeking God in prayer and His Word. God's challenge: "Make the most of the time because the days are evil" (Eph.5:16). True beauty is found in Jesus alone and in a life lived in "happy holiness" for God's glory!"

Chapter 13
Living Together

Being Sexually Active, Cohabitating, and Finding Your Mate

Dear Annie: My daughter, who's nineteen and away at college, confided in me that she is routinely "hooking up" and sees nothing wrong with it. Her latest guy is a two-week acquaintance and they're exploring moving in together. When I questioned her she got testy and said it's her life and "everybody's doin' it."

She's influencing her two younger sisters and I'm deeply disturbed. What should I do?"—Upset in Cleveland

Dear Upset: When you calm down, try to have a relaxed conversation with your daughter. She's perfectly normal and hopefully practices safe sex. Today if an "accident" does occur she can easily contact Planned Parenthood for reproductive services to take care of the problem. You can order or go online for my expert advice in these areas, as well as guide your other daughters on this wise path to sexual freedom and health.

This advice appears regularly in newspapers and magazines. Think of multitudes embracing it.

USA Today recently published the results of a national survey among 18- to 31-year-olds regarding cohabitation. A whopping seventy-six percent of young Americans said that living together before marriage is fine. The stark reality is that sixty-five percent of "altar–bound" singles—many of whom identify as "Christians"—now live together before marriage, a euphemism for a lifestyle of fornication.

Adding to the conversation on people "living together" are people making statements like the following: "Look, times have changed. We have to face certain realities of living in the 21st century. We're older... more mature... been divorced... not ready financially... providing parents to a child... benefiting from tax incentives...have peace that God understands our unique situation...After all, look how many celebrities and even 'Christians' are doing it."

Does it matter?

Let's answer the question from a Biblical perspective. Since God ordained marriage as the first institution, even before family, church, and government; took the initiative to bring the first man He created to his wife; filled the scriptures with practical principles and commands to ensure its success; and intended marriage to be an eternal picture of the beautiful relationship between Christ and His church (Eph. 5:31-32), we are not given the luxury to dishonor God by deviating from His divine blueprint for this sacred institution. Society does so to its own peril, something we are witnessing today in America.

> *"So I tell you this, and insist on it in the Lord, that you must no longer live as the Gentiles do, in the futility of their thinking. They are darkened in their understanding and separated from the life of God because of the ignorance that is in them due to the hardening of their hearts. Having lost all sensitivity, they have given themselves over to sensuality so as to indulge in every kind of impurity, with a continual lust for more" (Eph. 4:17-19).*

> *"But among you there must not be even a hint of sexual immorality, or of any kind of impurity, or of greed, because these are improper for God's holy people" (Eph. 5:3).*

Here's the deal: couples who are shacking up, living under one roof as a "pretend" married couple, are violating God's will for marriage no matter what their rationalization is economically, philosophically, or spiritually. It is a sinful pattern of behavior and must be repented of immediately. This includes those who say they are not "going all the way" sexually or "reside in separate rooms," deceived by thinking that they are immune to temptation or that neighbors don't form impressions based on appearances, nullifying their Christian witness. To ignore this will bring consequences—if not immediately, then eventually.

Having said the above, the good news is that our Creator has a plan to bring men and women together in the sacrament of holy matrimony! Soon my wife and I will celebrate 40 years of covenant marriage on the heels of her parents, who are at the 70-year mark. It began when we embraced the "Manufacturer's Handbook" (the Bible) and made a quality decision to carefully follow what it says. We invite you to follow us on this pathway to success.

Irv Gordon's Volvo just passed over the three million mark in mileage! He stated that the secret of his success was to follow from day one the specific plan in the manufacturer's handbook.

Consider the following scriptural insights regarding sex before marriage as well as how they guide any single man or woman to discover their God-ordained mate.

Ten Biblical Guidelines on Premarital Sex and Discovering God's Ideal Mate for Your Life

1. Make sure Jesus Christ is Lord over your life. There simply is no Biblical basis for saying "Jesus Christ is my Savior, but not my Lord." Lordship means uncompromising obedience to what He commands. The key is understanding who the Person is behind the commandments, and that He loves us and has nothing but the best in store for us.

2. Commit to live a life of moral purity. In the area of sex, God has put limitations on the display of physical affection prior to marriage because he wants us to experience the maximum benefits of a marriage built upon a proper foundation of love, respect, and covenantal commitment. God's plan is chastity (purity) before marriage and fidelity (loyalty) after marriage. Chastity is not a negative principle; it is keeping sex in the right place, for the right person, at the right time. Remember: *"There is a way that seems right to a man, but its end is the way of death" (Prov. 14:12).*

3. Trust your heavenly Father and live by faith. Christians are called to live by faith, without which we cannot please God (Heb. 11:6). Nothing so reflects the depth

of your trust in God as the choice of a life partner. Like Abraham did with Isaac, lay all preconceived notions and timetables on the altar and believe God that He will bring the right person at the right time.

4. Be intentional in the process. *"He who finds a wife finds a good thing and obtains favor from the Lord" (Prov. 18:22).* Everything begins by asking God to help you discern your mate, but then one cannot remain passive! A man has to provide for his household; therefore, discovering God's will for your career path is extremely important. No fellow has the right to invite a woman into his confusion!

Don't super-spiritualize things—make sure proper attention is given to cultivating both spiritual and physical disciplines, paying proper attention to physical appearance, demonstrating the attractiveness of a servant's heart, maintaining a healthy work/life balance, and learning basic time-management skills, as well as the basic principles of financial stewardship that will pay off handsomely in a marriage. Remember: marriage does not create problems so much as it reveals them!

A passage that God gave to my wife and me was, *"Prepare your work outside, get everything ready for yourself in the field, and after that build your house" (Prov. 24:27).*

5. Keep your focus on Jesus, not on finding a mate. When Paul was asked by single young men regarding this subject, he cautioned them to "live in a right way in undivided devotion to the Lord" (1 Cor. 7:35).

God does not want us getting all bent out of shape trying to discover our life partner. He wants us to first find rest and security in a relationship with Him. Walking around nervously like a turkey while going through the mental gymnastics of being preoccupied looking for our "perfect soulmate" (with our sixty-six-point check list from the hottest dating site) is not only exhausting but a clever tool of the enemy to take our eyes off of Jesus.

Right now, the most important question is not "Will I ever be married?" Instead, it's a two-part query: "What is God's will for my life now?" and then, "Am I doing it?"

Trying to hurry the process can cause lots of mistakes. Proverbs 19:2 tells us *"He who makes haste with his feet misses his way."*

6. Differentiate between loneliness and being alone. Feelings of loneliness are a normal part of life. Whether single or married, we all have times when we experience the emotion of loneliness. Yet for the Christian who has learned the secret of "abiding" in God as Jesus described in John 15, we can say as our Lord Himself said: *"You will leave me all alone. Yet I am not alone, for my Father is with me" (Jn 16:32).*

I still remember a conversation I had with a delightful woman who got married at the age of forty-one. She was beaming since she had waited so long for God to bring her into a covenant marriage with a tremendous man of God. She looked me in the eyes and smiled and told me these words, which I've never forgotten: "Larry, it would be far better to be single, in the will of God, and experience some moments of loneliness than to be married, out of the will of God, and experience a lifetime of chaos."

7. The New Testament tells us clearly that a Christian is only to marry another Christian:

   • "A wife is bound to her husband as long as he lives. If the husband dies, she is free to be married to whom she wishes, only in the Lord" (1 Cor. 7:39).

   • "How can two walk together, except they be agreed?" (Amos 3:3)

   • *"Have faith and love, and enjoy the companionship of those who love the Lord and have pure hearts" (2 Tim. 2:22 TLB).*

   God's people under the Old Covenant were forbidden to take foreign wives (Deut. 7:3) and repeatedly suffered the judgment of God when they disregarded this directive (see Ezra 10).

Genesis 24:1–4 directs the people of God not to take Canaanites for spouses. Someone has said that a Canaanite is someone who is selfish and lives to please himself as a non-believer. The word looks like "canine." In other words, a relationship with a Canaanite is puppy love that can be a prelude to a dog's life! Ask the multitudes who disregarded God's Word here and suffered terribly.

8. Celebrate the gift of singleness if God has uniquely chosen you. The overwhelming majority of people are designed to marry, have children and populate this world for the glory of God. Yet some people have a distinct calling to a life of singleness because of the unique task that God has for them.

In Matthew 19:12 Jesus described individuals who have this unique calling and receive it. Paul himself was a single man and told us of this special gift. He said by divine revelation that *"the one who can accept this should accept it" (1 Cor.7:7)*.

In the past generation, people said that if the Protestants had a pope he certainly would have been John Stott from England. Stott had tremendous impact and lived his life as a single man of God.

Think of the phenomenal ministry that Mother Teresa had in her lifetime as a single woman who voluntarily chose the path given to her as a single Christian.

As you read this, if you're wondering if you may have this gift yet have a burning desire to be married one day, let's get real and admit it—most likely, you ain't got it!

9. Concentrate on developing righteous friendships. Throughout my more than forty-three years of Christian ministry, I have discovered that the core component to a successful Christian marriage is a strong friendship base. Therefore, focus in on deepening wholesome,

godly friendships with members of both sexes to develop character, and broaden your ability to deal with
life situations and diverse people. At the same time remember that "bad company corrupts good morals" (1
Cor. 15:33), so steer clear of people and places that can
lead you down dangerous, compromising paths.

It is a sad reality that, while Christians have many
brothers and sisters in the Body of Christ, many really don't have genuine friends. As conditions continue to
disintegrate in our culture, increasingly we need to realize
how much we need to develop the gift of friendship, both
individually and in group situations, which have the benefit
of eliminating the pressure of the solitary "dating game."

*"Two are better than one, because they have a good re-
ward for their toil. For if they fall, one will lift up his
fellow; but woe to him who is alone when he falls and
has not another to lift him up" (Eccl 4:9-10).*

10. Enjoy Jesus! These were the dying words given me
by Eileen Wallis on her deathbed. She was the wife
of Arthur Wallis, one of the most influential Christian
leaders in Great Britain over the past century. Let's take
these words to heart whatever season of life we're in—
married or single.

Psalm 37:4 encourages us with this breathtaking promise: *"Delight
yourself in the Lord and He will give you the desires of your heart."*
If you'll have desires towards God, you'll gain desires from God!
You'll have assurance in your heart regarding your future and you
will discern His will, His way, and His timing regarding this major
area of your life. The seduction of being "free and sexually active"
or "living together before marriage" has ruined countless lives.

In order to know His choice you have to be able to hear His
voice! So stay close to Him and rest secure in your Bridegroom's
unconditional love for you as His bride. *"Trust in the Lord with all
your heart and lean not on your own understanding; in all your
ways acknowledge Him, and He will make your paths straight"
(Prov. 3:5-6).*

Chapter 14
Masturbation

"I'm Ashamed to Admit I Have a Problem With Masturbation"
"Larry, why include this topic in the Bullseye Challenge? It's not a major problem."

Really? Ted Roberts, author of a DVD series helping scores ensnared in pornography, states that "68% of Christian men view pornography and 50% of pastors view porn regularly." He bases this on a five-year national survey by Pure Desire Ministries. And what usually accompanies the watching of porn? *One guess.*

That leads us to an interesting question: "Was Jesus ever tempted sexually?"

This question was sheepishly and confidentially asked by a young man who took one of Christendom's premier preachers aside at a conference. Ern Baxter, whose message, "Thy Kingdom Come," is the best message I have ever heard in my forty-five years as a Christian, often shared the story. He knew that, as we age, we easily forget the raging hormones and intense sexual struggles of earlier years.

His answer?

"Young man, the Bible tells us that Jesus in His humanity can 'sympathize with our weaknesses as one who has been tempted in all things as we are, yet without sin'" (Heb. 4:15).

Hearing the answer, the young man breathed a sigh of relief, thanked Mr. Baxter, and quietly exited the room.

When I was a young, single man someone gave me a tract with the title "I Could Never Tell Anyone I Have a Problem With..." The cover depicted a dejected young man sitting with his head buried in his hands, staring at the ground, obviously in torment.

I thought it was significant that the title didn't finish the sentence, revealing the area of struggle. Solo sex is an uncomfortable topic that many people prefer to avoid.

In my library I have a 500+ page book by an internationally known Christian author on marriage and family life. The manual is a comprehensive reference book answering over 400 questions, yet to my knowledge, there is not even one reference to the subject of masturbation in this commentary.

I'm addressing it not to shock or be controversial or offend anyone, but rather to help people wrestling with this challenging issue. Certainly our sex-saturated culture has a multitude of voices sharing their perspective. Doesn't it make sense to have sound, scriptural counsel amidst all the ungodly advice bombarding us from every corner?

What follows will seem foolish and preposterous to pop-culture adherents, yet to those desiring to please God and live pure it brings peace, joy, and freedom. Ephesians 5:3 calls us *"God's holy people"* and says *"there must not be even a hint of sexual immorality, or of any kind of impurity... for it is shameful even to mention what the disobedient do in secret" (v. 12).*

If you don't think this really is much of a problem for scores of people in our society, I respectfully disagree. It's probably an overstatement when people say, "95% of people do it and the other 5% are liars," yet I'm persuaded that multitudes are just not aware of the extent of this behavior and how it's being aggressively promoted in society today:

- Pornography and erotic literature like *Fifty Shades of Grey* and the equally sensual sequel are rampant and fueling out-of-control sexual desires. This book alone sold over one hundred million copies worldwide and the movie grossed (no pun intended) megamillions.

- Sex-education classes and the World Health Organization encourage masturbation, plus abortion and homosexuality, to children and teens worldwide.

- Artists on YouTube and throughout the music industry gyrate while grabbing their crotches and celebrate pleasuring oneself, with titles such as "U and Ur Hand" (Pink), "Touch of my Hand" (Britney Spears), and "I Touch Myself" (the Divinyls).

- Conan O'Brien made a cultural icon out of the regularly featured "Masturbating Bear."

- Sex aids/toys are now advertised on mainstream TV, and in magazines and newspapers, and are available for purchase at your corner drugstore.

- Life-size "Love Dolls," recreating the appearance and texture of human females and males, are advertised; pushed on Facebook, Instagram, and Twitter; and highlighted on CBS's *2 Broke Girls* and HBO's *Real Sex*.

- Certain novelty stores in family malls now sell the "Masturbating Man" windup toy.

- "Christian" ministers seeking popularity and packed facilities proclaim, "Masturbation is actually a gift of God" (exact quote). Charlie Shedd, in his bestselling book of advice for teens, *The Stork is Dead*, said that masturbation is "the wise provision of a very wise Creator...He knew we'd need it!"

- Talk-show hosts and so-called experts on sexuality espouse their advice everywhere in our culture. Celebrating premarital sex and masturbation, most of them refer to their guru Alfred Kinsey and his "landmark" studies on sexual behavior. What they don't tell you is that historian James Jones, in his biography of Kinsey, stated that the pseudo-researcher was "a closeted homosexual and masochist who was obsessed with sex and driven by his own sexual demons..."

Here's the deal: Embracing a biblical worldview brings liberty and guilt-free sexuality.

1. There is both beauty and mystery in sex.
    Many Christians are ashamed to discuss what God is not ashamed to create and call "very good" (Gen 5:2). Satan seems to have engineered a conspiracy of silence on the subject of sex in many circles.
    Jesus said, *"The thief [Satan] comes only to steal and kill and destroy; I have come that they may have life, and have it to the full" (Jn. 10:10).* This includes a rich and fulfilling sexual experience when aligned with God's unchanging standards.
    According to Scripture, the wisest human being was King Solomon, who wrote over 1000 songs. His greatest song was the "Song of Songs," describing in poetic terms an amorous relationship between a pure maiden and her shepherd lover. It is a celebration of marital intimacy that includes:

    • Erotic dialogue throughout

    • Enjoyment of her breasts (7:7-8)

    • Intoxicating kissing (1:2)

    • Manual stimulation (2:6)

    • Sensual description of a lover (7:1-9)

    • Extensive use of highly sensuous and suggestive imagery involving the mouth, touch, and perfumed aromas

    Sexual pleasure is of divine origin, a gift from Almighty God, and enjoyed to the fullest when aligned with the will of God in covenant marriage.

2. While God *"richly provides us with everything for our enjoyment" (1 Tim. 6:17),* He commands us: *"Do not arouse or awaken love" (Sol. 8:4) before the proper time.*

    "There is a time for everything, and a season for every activity under heaven... a time to embrace and a time to

refrain... He has made everything beautiful in its time"
(Eccl 3:1-5).

My beautiful daughter, Melanie, lives and teaches God's liberating standard of moral purity. Keeping herself pure for years has not been easy, but long ago she made a quality decision to do things God's way and reaps the fruit of a healthy, guilt-free, abundant life.

Scripture always speaks approvingly of sexual pleasure as long as it is confined to married partners. God categorically and without exception prohibits premarital and extramarital activity.

"You will remember the instructions we gave you in the name of the Lord Jesus. God's plan is to make you holy, and that entails first of all a clean cut with sexual immorality. Every one of you should learn to control his body, keeping it pure and treating it with respect" (1 Thess. 4:2-4 Phillips).

A fire is warm and wonderful in a fireplace under control, but if that same fire is set loose it can burn down a house. Likewise, water is refreshing in the tap under control, but that same water rushing through a broken dam on a rampage can devastate an area and destroy human life. The difference? Control.

Our Creator's brilliant plan is for single men and women to develop the fruit of self-control (Gal. 5:23) prior to marriage by drawing on His grace and cooperating with His plan for sexual purity.

Do you know the number one reason why marriages break up? Sexual problems? Financial problems? Emotional problems? No. The primary reason is simply a lack of self-control! If a person can't control himself, he or she is vulnerable to multitudes of problems. Sexual problems break in. If a person can't control himself—financial problems crash in. It's the same with anger problems. Proverbs 25:28 reminds us, *"A man without self-control is like a city broken into and left without walls."*

In marriage one must often forego sexual activity because of sickness, pregnancy, or travel. Awhile back our daughter-in-law was expecting her third child and she and our son found themselves in this season. Self-controlled individuals who cultivate this character quality before marriage reap the dividends in marriage!

Obviously, another way that self-control is developed is by overcoming the inevitable temptations of masturbation.

3. Christians Are Not to be Mastered by Anything—that includes masturbation!

Scripture cautions us about individuals *"appealing to the lustful desires of sinful human nature"* promising "freedom" but bringing people into sexual bondage because *"a man is a slave to whatever has mastered him"* *(2 Pet. 2:18-19).*

We are to declare decisively and victoriously by faith: *"I will not be mastered by anything!"* (1 Cor. 6:12).

Jesus told us, *"I tell you the truth, everyone who sins is a slave to sin" (Jn. 8:34)*; yet right before this statement He encouraged us to continue in His word to *"know the truth, and the truth will set you free" (Jn 8:32).*

One lie regarding masturbation is expressed by comedian Jerry Seinfeld: "We all have to do it. It's part of our lifestyle, like shaving."

Another falsehood believed by the masses is: "I'm trapped. I can't stop. I'll never break free. God hates me and I know He'll punish me. I've done this too much and there's no way that God could ever forgive me."

Another lie: "There's nothing sinful or harmful about masturbation. It's just a natural way to relieve sexual tension and pleasure oneself."

Still another lie: "Habitual masturbation is akin to the unforgivable sin. Plus it causes deafness, blindness, epilepsy, acne, brain damage, sterility, and impotence. In women it damages childbearing capability."

All of the above are Biblically and/or scientifically false. Some of these myths led parents to severely punish their children if caught in the act and others told their children that God would strike them dead like Onan (Gen. 38:8-10) for playing with themselves. (Note: For centuries people mistakenly thought the "sin of Onan" was masturbation. This narcissistic man, whose older brother died without fathering any children, was covenantally responsible to produce offspring but didn't want a child to get any inheritance before he did. So he practiced *coitus interruptus* and God put him to death for his callous selfishness.)

Because pastors and parents were misinformed and confused about what they perceived to be this "wicked vice," they magnified this act above all others, shamed offenders and even purchased chastity belts, aluminum mitts, or handcuffs to lock their children down at bedtime!

4. Simple and Straightforward Truths About the Subject

- The term "masturbation" is derived from two Latin words: "manus" (hand) and "turbatio" (agitation). Allow me a slight bit of sanctified comic relief here by injecting that this is not the meaning behind Ecclesiastes 9:10: "Whatever your hand finds to do, do it with all your might..."

- The term does not appear anywhere in the Bible, neither does it make any direct statement about masturbation. Because the Bible does not explicitly condone or condemn masturbation, we must look to Biblical principles for guidance and avoid dogmatic pronouncements on the subject. Some believe it is always a sin; others see it as wrong because it's less than God's ideal, but think that there may be some exceptions; there are those who view it in a neutral way as a matter of individual conscience; and, as referenced earlier, some see it as a "gift from God."

- Previously we clarified the Genesis 38:9–11 account of Onan. Other Old-Testament references are Leviticus 15:16–17; Deut. 23:10-11, and Lev. 22:4, which could be the result of this activity or a nocturnal emission (natural, nighttime release of fluid while sleeping). Here God gave directions not because anything was sinful or "dirty" but for hygiene and emphasizing self-control. Similar guidance was given for women during their monthly cycle.

- In the New Testament we find a passage similar to the one previously mentioned (1 Thess. 4:3-5), also underscoring self-control (1 Cor.7:1-5), and also emphasizing the marriage relationship as a practical solution and safeguard for struggling singles who "burn with passion" (v. 9). With our society overwhelmingly saying "Indulge yourself," God tells us "Control yourself!"

- •As holy/set-apart disciples of Jesus Christ told to "*set before my eyes no unclean thing*" *(Ps. 101:3)* (I have this passage on a card affixed to our television) and to never "*look lustfully upon a woman*" *(Matt. 5:28),* obviously we're to avoid sexually explicit images that fuel passions often leading to masturbation. Pornography is actually material to be read or seen with one hand, that is, as an accompaniment to solo sex.

- The same goes for entertaining illicit sexual fantasies in the mind that lead to instant gratification. Therefore, aware that the "*heart is deceitful above all things and desperately wicked...*" *(Jer. 17:9).* Let's be brutally honest: Is masturbation a holy and honorable way to glorify God, cultivate self-control and avoid sexual uncleanness?

- For individuals in unique circumstances and seasons of life, we must ask God for wisdom in righteously dealing with legitimate sexual desire, e.g., widows or widowers reflecting on memories of their deceased spouse;

living with an incapacitated mate; or a husband or wife away for extended periods of time in military service, imprisonment or lengthy business/ministry trips.

• Finally, for those who ask the inevitable question, "What if I feel helpless or too often slip?" Remember that we defeat temptation from a position of victory, not one of trying to achieve it! Jesus Christ came to provide us not only forgiveness of sin but liberation from its power! We have the ability to sin but no longer the obligation.

Like Job, make a "covenant with your eyes (Job 31:1). "Flee evil"—don't flirt with it. If you allow Satan to get his foot in the door, he'll come in and try to destroy your whole house! Spend consistent time in the Word of God ("How can a young man keep his way pure? By living according to your Word"—Ps. 119:9); grow in character and self-control through godly accountability with other like-minded Christians of the same sex; and affirm by faith your liberation from sin's compulsive power.

As a young man I put on my hallway mirror a scriptural statement to confess regularly. It's from Romans 6:6–7, a verse that I personalized to build my faith and walk as an overcomer. Little by little my mind was renewed to believe this fact. "I don't have to serve sin today. I have been set free!"

If you're tired of being Satan's Pinocchio, with his pulling the strings and manipulating you to walk in defeat, condemnation, and uncleanness, then repent of any passivity and reject the lie that this temptation is too difficult to defeat. No Christian should ever be ashamed to admit they have a problem with masturbation. There's hope and victory in Jesus!

Claim forgiveness from our holy, yet merciful Father. Don't plan to fall, but if you do immediately arise to repent and continue your journey to glorify God. There is hope and victory in Jesus!

> *"No temptation has seized you except what is common to man. And God is faithful; He will not let you be tempted beyond what you can bear. But when you are tempted, He will also provide a way out so that you can stand up under it" (1 Cor. 10:13).*

Chapter 15
Affairs

Steering Clear Of Adultery's Subtle Seduction
It seems that not a week goes by when we don't read the account of some high-profile pastor, politician, celebrity, or local leader who has succumbed to the seduction of adultery. Add to this the reports that flow in the office, on the campus, or in our neighborhoods, and it makes you just shake your head and shudder, asking, "When is this going to stop?"

In addition to the shameful example exhibited by the Christian community, consider the names of key people in our culture who have gone down the path of adultery in recent years:

- Steve Croft: *60 Minutes* journalist and TV personality

- Gen. David Petraeus: Four-star general and former head of the CIA and armed forces in Afghanistan and Iraq; resigned at the age of 60 due to an extramarital affair.

- Eliot Spitzer: Former governor of New York; caught in an extramarital affair at the age of 48

- Mark Sanford: Former governor of South Carolina; caught in an extramarital affair at the age of 49.

- John Edwards: Former presidential candidate; admitted, at the age of 56, to having an extramarital affair that included fathering a child.

- Brian Dunn: Former CEO of Best Buy; resigned at the age of 52 due to alleged personal misconduct, later revealed to be a close relationship with a female employee.

- Harry Stonecipher: Former president and CEO of Boeing; resigned at the age of 69 due to an improper relationship with a Boeing executive.

- Chris Kubasik: Former president of Lockheed Martin; resigned at the age of 51 due to conducting a close, personal relationship with a subordinate employee.

This is just a partial list, and only of those who got caught!

Scripture warns us that prior to the return of our Lord Jesus Christ, wickedness will increase. In our sex-saturated society, all of us must be on guard against the "wiles of the devil" (Eph. 6:11) in the realm of moral impurity. Remember that David was not a young man when he succumbed to sexual sin. Most commentators believe that his age was around 51 years old.

First Corinthians 10:12 warns us, *"So, if you think you are standing firm, be careful that you don't fall!" (NIV)*. Gordon MacDonald, former president of InterVarsity Christian Fellowship and author of *Magnificent Marriage* and *The Effective Father*, told us after his moral failure that he neglected to heed the counsel of Oswald Chambers, who said, *"An unguarded strength is a double weakness."*

Thank God that Gordon humbled himself, submitted to the discipline that was necessary, and for years now has been restored as an effective leader.

The Challenge of Living Chaste in Our Culture

It doesn't matter if you're a male or female, single, divorced, or married. We are all living in a culture characterized by an explosion of three things:

1. The elimination of restraints and sexual taboos;

2. Erotic stimuli that bombards us everywhere; and

3. The pervasive encouragement to indulge yourself rather than the Biblical standard to control yourself.

Dr. Ted Roberts is trying to combat the avalanche of pornography flooding our churches with a DVD series advertised with provocative statements like "68% of Christian men view pornography" and "50% of pastors view porn regularly." He bases this on a five-year national survey conducted by Pure Desire Ministries entitled "Porn Usage in the Evangelical Church."

Paul Coelho, one of the most influential writers of our time, just released his latest book called *Adultery*, which deals with this theme in our society today.

In case you haven't heard, the latest cultural trend being pushed is something called "sugar dating" where primarily younger women trade sexual companionship for money given by older, oftentimes married, wealthy men. The documentary *Daddies Date Babies* surveys this development and explains how many millennial girls engage in this activity to get quick cash and pay off their debts!

There is a movie called *Men, Women and Children* that portrays how sex is pulling at us from every side in today's digital age. *USA Today* reviewed it and stated: "What's happening to us in the process? With porn at the ready on 'incognito' tabs, BDSM a jarring go-to for teens and Ashley Madison ads winking over one-click affairs, where are we headed?"

In an article in *The Christian Post* entitled "The Defining Moment Between Attraction and Sexual Sin," the author confessed that "after living 19 years free from dealing with sexual attraction outside my marriage, I find myself experiencing those old familiar triggers once again. YIKES!"

Gordon McDonald relates how he once was asked by a businessman, if Satan were to "blow him out of the water," how would he do it? Gordon responded, "He'd never get me in the area of morality. I'm just too strong there. It would have to be somewhere else."

It would do us all good to regularly meditate on the scripture *"So if you think you are standing firm, be careful that you don't fall! No temptation has overtaken you except what is common to mankind. And God is faithful; He will not let you be tempted beyond what you*

*can bear. But with the temptation will provide the way of escape to
bear up under it" (1 Cor. 10:12-13).*

Wouldn't it also do us good to consider the reasons why women
and men get involved in sexually inappropriate or adulterous
relationships? If we identify some signposts leading to the shipwreck,
hopefully we'll steer clear before it's too late. Since much of this occurs
in the middle years of peoples' lives, let's consider the following by
zeroing in on men (although women go down a similar path.) Even
if you're younger, remember "to be forewarned is to be forearmed."

*Seven Reasons Why Middle-aged Men Get Involved in Sexual
Immorality*

1. A heart issue: they've never really submitted totally
to Jesus Christ as Lord and then become established
in an authentic local church for ongoing nurturing and
support.

2. An unhealthy fear that time is fleeting and they must
"grab the gusto" and experience whatever sexual pleasure remains before it's too late.

3. Sensing a lessening of physical attractiveness for their
spouse and possible floating bitterness that she is "letting herself go," thinking it's all right to be attracted to
and involved with other available women.

4. Because a spouse is uninterested in sexual activity,
maybe experiencing menopause, thinking God understands and "gives a pass" to engage in extramarital sexual behavior.

5. As children have grown and left for college or marriage,
there's simply more time for other pursuits, which can
include exploring new realms of sexual relationships.

6. Greater financial prosperity enables discretionary income to be tapped for recreation, hobbies, gadgets, and
why not some sexual pursuits?

7. Whereas resolving relationship conflicts quickly was once
a priority, now laziness and selfishness rules, allowing the

marriage to drift and a gulf to widen—a setup for Satan's alternative.

The subtlety of sexual sin was seen in the entrapment of David with Bathsheba. We must be on guard for *external* danger signals in relating to the opposite sex (growing dependence on someone; receiving affirmation and praise; listening to complaints about loneliness; receiving gifts; enjoying physical contact...) as well as *internal* danger signals (regularly thinking about a person; comparing the person to one's spouse; finding excuses to be around the individual; having sexual fantasies about the person; scheming ways to be alone with them; sharing marital problems with them; exploring Facebook contacts; keeping "articles of affection" from an old flame...).

In these challenging times, it is critical to be aggressive in putting to death fleshly impulses and guarding our minds. May we discern any subtle signs of attraction and seduction and radically avoid associations where we might be drawn into temptation.

No matter what our age, let's resolve to be aggressive in avoiding temptation and attacking sin when it first rears its ugly head! *"I pursued my enemies and overtook them; I did not turn back till they were destroyed. I crushed them so that they could not rise; they fell beneath my feet" (Ps. 18:37-38).*

Personally, I have been married faithfully for almost 40 years, and my wife's parents have been married for 70 years. Among 63 family members (children, grandchildren and great-grandchildren), there have been no divorces and no cases of adultery—thanks be to God!

I have learned a lot from those who surround me. Besides their wonderful example, I've also had a healthy dose of the fear of God instilled in me. And to keep that healthy fear of God ever present, I engage in a regular spiritual discipline that I've passed on to multitudes in my more than forty-three years of full-time ministry and pass on to you below.

The 25 Consequences of an Adulterous Relationship
I keep handy a list of what can happen to an individual who stupidly yields to adultery. I read through this slowly and prayerfully on a somewhat regular basis. I make copies and pass it along to others. I'd like to share it with you and pray you do likewise. I credit Randy

Alcorn and Alan Hlavka as the two Christian leaders who formulated most of this list decades ago.

The Bible and my conscience strongly warn me about going down the path to adultery. Whenever I feel particularly vulnerable to sexual temptation or sense I'm being deceived, I will review what effects my action can have:

1. Grieving the God who created and redeemed me

2. Causing the sacred name of my Lord Jesus to be mocked and ridiculed

3. Having to look Jesus, the righteous Judge, in the face on Judgment Day to give an account for my actions

4. Following in the tragic footsteps of those whose immorality forfeited their position and reputation

5. Inflicting untold hurt on my wife, my best friend and loyal companion

6. Losing my wife's respect, trust, and confidence

7. Hurting my beloved children and possibly disillusioning them to Christianity for life

8. Destroying my example and credibility with my children and probably nullifying both present and future efforts to teach them to obey God

9. Perhaps losing my wife and my children forever through a divorce and relocation

10. Causing a potential of lifetime shame to my wider family name

11. Losing self-respect and a clean conscience

12. Forming memories and flashbacks that could haunt me for the rest of my life, as well as hinder future intimacy with my wife

13. Wasting years of career training and experience should I forfeit my job

14. Forfeiting the effect of years of witnessing to others and reinforcing their distrust for Christians

15. Undermining the faithful example and hard work of other Christians in the Christian community

16. Bringing great pleasure to Satan, the enemy of God and all that is good

17. Risking very real physical harm from a jealous boyfriend or spouse

18. Heaping judgment and endless difficulty on the person with whom I committed adultery

19. Bearing potential physical consequences of STDs like gonorrhea, syphilis, chlamydia, herpes, and AIDS; infecting my wife and causing sterility, deformity, or even death

20. Possibly causing pregnancy, with the personal and financial implications, including a lifelong reminder of my sin

21. Heaven forbid if the unborn baby was aborted and we were haunted by this fact all the days of my life

22. Living with debilitating fear and guilt, maybe even blackmail, until the sin was exposed

23. Invoking shame and lifelong embarrassment on myself

24. Experiencing long-standing mental and emotional distress plus sexual baggage, sleeplessness, depression, migraines, obesity, etc.

25. Long-standing financial repercussions.

Let's resolve that we will not only consider these very real consequences on a regular basis but will take seriously what it means to be involved in a covenant marriage as Christians.

Here's the deal, as God says it best:

As for other matters, brothers and sisters, we instructed
you how to live in order to please God, as in fact you are

living. Now we ask you and urge you in the Lord Jesus to do this more and more. For you know what instructions we gave you by the authority of the Lord Jesus. It is God's will that you should be sanctified: that you should avoid sexual immorality; that each of you should learn to control your own body in a way that is holy and honorable, not in passionate lust like the pagans, who do not know God; and that in this matter no one should wrong or take advantage of a brother or sister. The Lord will punish all those who commit such sins, as we told you and warned you before. For God did not call us to be impure, but to live a holy life. Therefore, anyone who rejects this instruction does not reject a human being but God, the very God who gives you his Holy Spirit (1 Thess. 4:1-8).

Chapter 16
Divorce and Remarriage

What Did Jesus Really Say?

The oldest brother of Jesus Christ and the leader of the first Jerusalem council was called a "pillar" in the church (Gal 2:9). He was also selected by God to give us this very wise and practical advice: "My dear brothers, take note of this: everyone should be quick to listen, slow to speak and slow to become angry..." (James 1:19).

When a couple is beginning to entertain thoughts of divorce, they usually spin in the opposite direction. As matters escalate it isn't long before papers are being signed, family and friends take sides, and the date in court comes and goes as another marriage dissolves.

If you or someone you know is headed in this direction, can we push the pause button and ponder some things before it's too late? It does take humility but the Lord also inspired James to caution, "God resists the proud but gives grace to the humble" (James 4:6). If there's one person in all the universe you don't want opposing you, it's God!

As my wife and I celebrate our fortieth wedding anniversary, we'd like to share some thoughts regarding divorce. There's no need to quote the dismal statistics in our nation today; let's just take a look at it from God's viewpoint and see if we can discover some solutions.

If you're a young person who's single, take heed to what is God's perspective in this area so you'll understand not to take this topic lightly. In another line from the blockbuster movie *Jurassic World*, a teen brushes off his parents' impending divorce by snidely telling his crying younger brother, "It's okay. All my friends' parents are divorced."

Now if you are reading this having been through a divorce, don't succumb to condemnation, but rather reflection. Were you an unbeliever? Were you in a backslidden state and have since returned to God? If you did not have any Biblical grounds for divorce, have you thoroughly repented and consecrated yourself to obey God without reservation? Have you learned the lessons God wants to teach you in your journey as you pursue a fresh start?

If you're currently married to an unbeliever, please jettison thoughts like "How can I get out of this?" and replace them with God's Word that unbelievers "may be won over without talk by the behavior of their wives..." (1 Pet. 3:1). This applies to a man with an unbelieving wife also.

Finally, in all that follows, remember that believing prayer is critical. "Everything is possible to him who believes" (Mk 9:23) comes from the lips of our Lord Jesus Christ, not Dr. Phil or Oprah! We have seen miracles of marriages' restoration (even couples remarrying each other after divorcing!) when Christians humbly submit to God rather than erratic emotions and irrational thinking.

A Biblical Worldview on Divorce and Remarriage
There are three Biblical grounds for divorce and remarriage:

1. Ongoing and unrepentant adultery (Matt. 19:9).

2. Abandonment by an unbeliever (1 Cor.7:15)—actual physical and longstanding desertion (and some would also add persistent physical abuse/violence that reveals "breaking faith"/abandonment of any semblance of true faith as grounds for separation and later possible divorce)

   "'I hate divorce,' says the Lord God of Israel, 'and I hate a man's covering himself with violence as well as with his garment,' says the Lord Almighty. So guard yourself in your spirit, and do not break faith" (Mal. 2:16 NIV).

3. A former marriage with subsequent divorce as a non-Christian. *"If anyone be in Christ, he is a new creation: old things have passed away, behold all things become new" (2 Cor. 5:17).*

Yes, there sometimes is a legitimate and Biblical basis for a divorce. Yet this fact does not mean they're a first recourse or an easy way out of a situation in which God is endeavoring to mature our character as we submit in obedience rather than convenience.

God hates divorce (Mal 2:16), but there is something He hates even more: adultery. This is why He allows it as grounds to nullify a sacred marriage covenant. God hates divorce, not divorced people, because of what it does to men and women and children and families and a nation and a generation. It's like when we say we hate cancer but we don't hate people with cancer.

In our society we've trivialized and minimized divorce. It's a sad reality that it has become an acceptable solution to a couple's difficulties in marriage. What God is calling us to do is to change our mind about divorce, as well as to stop advising it as a quick way out of the problems couples inevitably face in marriage.

When the Pharisees tried to trap Jesus regarding divorce and Mosaic law, He answered that divorce was permitted because of the "hardness of their hearts" but He renewed the original standard by saying "it was not this way from the beginning" (Matt 19:7-8).

A Christian marriage is different from what the world puts forth as its concept of marriage. God's design for marriage is not like "high school dating" or as a contract to be dissolved when the going gets tough. God ordained marriage as a covenant—a sacred and binding vow between one man and one woman with God at the center for all of one's life.

Marriage is not intended to be a fifty-fifty proposition. The biblical view of marriage is giving up one's self one hundred percent for your husband or wife. Contrary to what much of our society believes, love is not merely a fleeting emotion or sexual attraction but an unselfish choice for the greatest good of the other person.

When my wife and I entered into a marriage covenant almost forty years ago this April 10, we stood before a thousand people and declared our intention to enter a covenant marriage. The message given by the minister focused in on the elements of a covenant and we exchanged our Biblical vows, one of which was "Divorce is not an option."

Over 14,000 days later, in spite of incredible adversity, trials, and challenges, we're still happily standing together to the glory of God! Never once in all of those years have we ever even uttered the word "divorce" to each other in the midst of our probably thousands of conflicts.

We are bound together by God and our vows made in the presence of multitudes of witnesses. In the face of massive problems we have simply drawn upon the grace of God, obeyed the scripture on how to resolve conflicts, and done our best to "never let the sun go down on our anger" as the Bible instructs (Eph. 4:26). And when we've had times of extreme tension, being in the midst of what felt like a "nuclear war," we humbled ourselves and drew upon trusted, mature Christian friends to whom we are accountable to help us break through the impasse to victory.

We hope you will follow our example. It's not that we are special. We are simply mutual servants of the Lord and one another who desire to honor God in marriage and our family. In the very core of your being, isn't that what motivates you?

My wife's parents have been married for seventy years! Amongst their eight children and their children's children there are seventeen marriages and yet no divorces. Why? We simply adhere to the Biblical pattern.

Not long ago my wife and I sat down and counted the married family and friends we have been close to in our lifetime. Of approximately 140 couples, we discovered that there were a number who lost their spouses to death but only one who has gone through a divorce! I don't say this to impress the reader but to make the point strongly that these folks align with the Word of God on marriage and by His grace walk it out, reaping the success resulting from obedience. Isn't that what you want?

Christian marriage is not the absence of conflict but the overcoming of it! If you can stand the pull, God will pull you through. But will you submit to Him and His Word or succumb to your emotions when the heat is on?

Someone once asked the late Ruth Graham if, in her marriage to Billy Graham, she ever thought about divorce. "Divorce? No. Now murder....," she chuckled.

Remember, love is not primarily a feeling! It is an unselfish choice for the greatest good of the other person. So if you are tempted to say "I don't think I love my spouse anymore," then it's time to turn things around by forgiving and learning to love that person Biblically.

A number of years ago I sat in my living room with "Gary," who said he was going to divorce his wife because he didn't feel he loved her anymore. Because I had the privilege to sit under the teaching ministry of the great guru of all counselors, Jay Adams, I knew exactly what to do.

After explaining to him that Biblical love for his spouse was not predicated upon fleeting emotions, I shared with him the verse in which husbands are commanded (not suggested) to love their wives (Eph. 5:25). He promptly told me he didn't "feel" he could do that.

So next I reminded him that God commands us to love our neighbor as ourselves and that his wife was obviously his closest neighbor. Again he quickly retorted that he didn't "feel" that was still possible.

Finally I looked him straight in the eye and said, "Gary, God even commands you to love your enemies! If that's how you are currently viewing her, you still have no escape route."

My brother really was trapped. He either was going to learn to love his wife whether he felt like it or not or choose to disregard God's Word and suffer the inevitable consequences, which I'm sad to say he did.

If you or someone you know is facing the temptation to "throw in the towel" and just get a divorce, will you take some time to step back, reflect on what's been said here, and ask God for the grace to do whatever is necessary to preserve the marriage? If you will honor God and His Word, He will intervene in ways that will amaze you!

Let me conclude by quoting from a newsletter published a number of years back by Dr. James Dobson when he was leading the Focus on the Family ministry. He shared the results of a scientific study entitled, "Does Divorce Make People Happy?" conducted by the Institute for American Values. The findings were noteworthy because they "debunked the modern myth that someone in a troubled marriage is faced with a choice between either staying in a miserable relationship or getting a divorce to be more happy."

This study revealed "a full two-thirds of the unhappily married spouses who stayed married were actually happier five years later! Among those who initially rated their marriages as 'very unhappy' but remained together, nearly eighty percent considered themselves 'happily married' and 'much happier' five years later."

Surprisingly, the opposite is found to be true for those who divorced. The Institute for American Values study confirmed that divorce frequently fails to make people happy because, while it might provide a respite from the pain associated with a bad marriage, it also introduces a host of complex new emotional and psychological difficulties over which the parties involved have little control. They include child-custody battles, emotionally scarred children, and economic hardships ("Family News" from Focus on the Family, Dr. James Dobson, September 2002).

As we continue our "Bullseye Challenge," may we have fresh resolve to honor God's standards regarding marriage. We invite you to follow us as we follow Christ in covenant marriage. Perseverance really does pay off! Remember that Jesus Himself told us that it is those *"who hear the word, retain it, and by persevering produce a crop" (Luke 8:15).*

Chapter 17
Sexting

Harmless Youthful Fun?

You're sitting in the Publix parking lot at dusk and notice the unsupervised 12-year-old riveted to his iPhone with his wide-eyed friend looking on.

Walking through the mall you see three teen girls seemingly oblivious to surroundings as they stroll together, each focused on their phones.

Munching their curly fries at Arby's, each of five youths are simultaneously engaged with their phones.

Stopping at the intersection you glance over and observe a preteen in the backseat, basking in the glow of her phone.

Mobile phones and teens are everywhere. The question is: "What are they looking at?" And if you're a young person, shoot straight: do you indulge in this practice of "sexting"?

"Vamping" refers to teenagers staying up after hours and engaging socially and possibly sharing sexually related items.

"Sexting" refers to transmitting provocative sexual images of oneself to others.

If your son or daughter has access to an iPhone, are you absolutely sure there's no questionable activity going on? More importantly, do you know how to protect your children from the onslaught they face in today's technological revolution?

In recent days *Atlantic Monthly*, the *Washington Post*, NBC News, *PBS NewsHour*, and other news outlets are recognizing the rising tide of sexting among youth in our culture. We ignore these warnings to our peril. Let's survey the situation so we are both informed and prepared as young people and parents.

Seven Realities Regarding Sexting

1. Our culture encourages sharing of both information and images freely, including those of a sexual nature.

2. Nude or nearly nude pictures and themes are common-place in ads, Instagram or on YouTube. Miley Cyrus, Nikki Minaj, Beyoncé, Rihanna, and other "strippers" masquerade as dancers. Hot groups like "Nude Beach" fan the flames while Maybelline runs full-page ads heralding the idea to "Dare to Go Nude!" Shamefully explicit Victoria's Secret displays hit us on every side— television, posters, and provocative magazine layouts.

3. The message is clear: Throw off restraints; don't hold back; show and enjoy what you got!

4. Exchanging naked pictures on iPhones or in other places is not viewed as unusual; we're being told it's "normal" and is "happening all the time."

5. In a recent *Washington Post* article on this topic by psychologist and professor Elizabeth Englander, the "expert" calls us to stop demonizing teen sexting. She says that in most cases it's "harmless" and a "normal part of a teen's sexual development." It's kinda like "I'll show you mine if you show me yours!"

6. Research studies reveal that forty percent of teenagers have posted or sent sexually provocative messages. Over ten percent of thirteen- to sixteen-year-old teen girls admit sending or receiving sexually explicit messages.

7. Seventy percent of young people acknowledge that their sexting is with a boyfriend/girlfriend.

8. Fifty-five percent admit, no matter what they say to others, that they share content with more than one person. The average guy has little chance of discretely deleting that "juicy" picture with such bragging rights available the next time he's with his buds!

9. Thirty-three percent do it to "feel attractive/sexy"— girls send more sexual images than guys.

10. Twelve percent do it because they are pressured/manipulated.

In this month's *Atlantic* magazine, the cover story on "Why Kids Sext" visited a high school of 1450 where students surveyed said they believed that anywhere from sixty to eighty percent of their classmates sext. Some of the more significant excerpts include:

- "The speed in which teens have incorporated the practice of sharing naked pictures of themselves into their mating rituals has taken society by surprise."

- "This is my life and my body and I can do whatever I want with it!" declared one girl.

- In another high school surveyed, twenty-eight percent of sophomores and juniors said they sent naked pictures of themselves and thirty-one percent asked someone to send them one.

- The act of sending sexually explicit material through mobile phones does not just entail bikinis and scantily-clad girls in bras and panties but frontal nudity, individuals performing sex acts, and group sex.

"Is this really just harmless activity for young people, a playful stage to pass through?"

Last year, Audrey Pott, a curvy sophomore at Saratoga High School in California, wore a low-cut top and a miniskirt to school and got messages on Facebook like "U WERE ONE HORNY MOFU!"

Earlier she had deceived her parents regarding a "sleepover" when it was, in actuality, a party with young people where she got drunk and guys took compromising pictures of her and later circulated them on the phone.

No big deal? On that very first day of school she came home from school, went into her bedroom, and moments later, her mother found her hanging dead in the bathroom from the experience.

What's amazing to consider is what publication probably did the longest feature on this incident—none other than *Rolling Stone*! The herald of hedonism that celebrates drugs, booze, rebellion, and anything goes, and regularly features pictures of "cool" celebrities smoking dope, tells the story in all its gory details.

In another school, two popular girls persuaded an autistic boy to share pictures of his privates with them, which they forwarded to schoolmates as a prank.

In Virginia, a thirteen-year-old girl posted her naked picture on a website and had grown men show up at her house.

Guys have learned to manipulate by threatening to send out naked pictures of their girlfriends unless given the sexual favors they demand. Others have become ensnared in sexual trafficking through such intimidation.

Imagine your naïve, just-developing daughter looking in the mirror and repeatedly wondering, "Am I attractive? Do I look sexy? Guys at school say girls who don't sext aren't cool, they're stuck up; is that me?"

Then some Justin Bieber guy on whom she's had a "crush" texts her when her parents are asleep and she's exiting the shower. BAE, WYD? "Getting ready for bed" WHAT ARE YA WEARING? "Wraparound towel" WOW! YOU ALWAYS LOOK SO HOT. BET YOU'RE SMOKIN' HOT NOW! "Really?" TAYLOR SWIFT'S GOT NOTHIN ON YOU. YOU'RE ALONE—SHOOT ME A PIX. JUST FOR ME. I'LL DELETE IT... PROMISE. COME ON, I'M PERSISTENT BAE!

Vulnerable. Gullible. Alone. Late. Why not...once... Just for him?

Practical Guidance for Parents (And for Young People to Know and Uphold)

1. Pray to God for divine protection, discernment, and wisdom. Your assignment is to equip and empower

them to make wise decisions on their own; help them understand choices and long-term effects.

2. Make sure you are meaningfully involved in a community of believers with like-minded parents who share a Biblical worldview on sexuality and parenting.

3. Be engaged with cell phone usage and monitoring and the safeguards available today. Many wise parents have initiated reasonable curfews in the evening regarding cell phone usage.

4. Reject the notion that, in the teen years, parents step back rather than stay involved. In this season they need you more than ever!

5. Remember that you're first and foremost a parental authority, not a buddy or friend. Talk-show host Kelly Ripa shared recently about her thirteen-year-old daughter having cell phone privileges curtailed: "I don't care if she doesn't like me. I'm not trying to be her friend. I'm her mom!"

6. Teach your children that there is a mystique to sex that's God-ordained. While the culture seduces us to "indulge yourself," the Holy Scriptures direct us, "Control yourself."

   "Young women… I charge you: do not stir up or awaken love until the appropriate time" (Song of Sol. 8:4 CSB).

7. "For everything there is a season, and a time for every matter under heaven… a time to embrace, and a time to refrain from embracing… He has made everything beautiful in its time" (Eccl. 3:1, 5b, 11 RSV).

8. Clearly and convincingly explain that there are very severe legal consequences for sexting. In some states teenagers can be charged with a felony, given a twenty-year prison sentence, and registered as a sex offender for life. Continue with a very honest conversation about ruined reputations, humiliation, depression, revenge tactics, sexual predators,

and opening doors to pornography, homosexuality, and eventually even suicide.

Remember your normal sexual curiosity as a youth? It's by divine design. But if parental authorities are not present to instruct, steer, and oversee it in young people, it becomes like a fire out of control, leading to disastrous consequences. In today's cultural morass, we have no more options except to hit this head on and trust God for His protection.

Here's the deal: There simply are no easy solutions or shortcuts anymore. The United States of America desperately needs a transformative revival. As we await that divine intervention let us pray and stay close together as families did in the time of Nehemiah when the city of God was being restored.

Chapter 18
Gay Children

If Your Child Told You, "I'm Gay!" What Would You Do?
While this chapter is directed more towards parents, I encourage every young person to read it. Many so-called "experts" and leaders are intellectually dishonest with you and you need to know the truth. In our Bullseye Challenge we need to know what to say and do if our child tells us they're "coming out as gay" or if it happens with your brother or sister.

Thirty-five years ago at an outdoor Christian festival, I made an erroneous statement for which I was sued for twenty million dollars. Thank God the case was settled. The nightmare revolved around the mistaken notion that the author of a pop psychology book was dead. The book was called *I'm OK, You're OK*.

That catchy title is repeated oftentimes to this day in counseling parents how to handle a son or daughter revealing that they are gay or lesbian. "Don't be judgmental. Convey unconditional love. Accept them as they are. Realize they're born this way. Reassure them you're okay and they're okay in whatever sexual identity they choose."

Understanding the Situation
A Catholic Republican governor states unequivocally that he believes that homosexuality is not a sin and that people are simply

born that way. He speaks at major conservative conferences and many believe he is a viable presidential candidate. His unbiblical thinking is typical of scores in our culture today.

In addition to influential politicians, advice columnists, celebrities, talk show hosts, sports figures, famous singers, educators, counselors, and even ministers affirm and celebrate individuals of all ages who are "courageous and honest to come out" as gay, lesbian, transgender, or bisexual.

Little children are featured in YouTube videos, in DVDs and in books like *It's Perfectly Normal* (with more than one million copies in print) that are used in schools across America to educate and convince children from kindergarten up that it's okay to be gay. "I was really scared of coming out at an early age... It was soothing to hear teachers and faculty at school letting me know that it's okay. Just to know that I had that support and to hear from other people at my school that it was okay, I think it really lifted a burden off my shoulders." (From "It's Elementary. Talking about Gay Issues in School").

In Boston a major conference of LGBT leaders and activists convened to discuss strategies for aggressively blanketing elementary, middle, and high schools across the nation. Workshops and seminar sessions were held to lay out plans for continuing to establish gay clubs in every school, promote "Days of Silence" to stifle negative comments, and more effectively disseminate information to educate, as well as inspire, youth about the LGBT lifestyle.

This full-court propaganda press is unprecedented and of epic proportions. States are now enacting laws to prevent counselors from helping a child struggling with same-sex attraction know that they can change. It is coming at our children from schools, media, and political realms, including the prominent placement of gay, lesbian, bisexual, and transgender people in TV, music, and films.

To compound the situation, we have influential ministers who, in their churches, on the radio, and in TV interviews, downplay the entire gay issue and smile, explaining that it's not really part of their ministry. Their silence is deafening as they prefer to remain quiet and noncontroversial while not "offending" people they're trying to draw into their growing ministry.

Houston's lesbian mayor passed a law—which was later overturned—making all public bathrooms, showers, and dressing rooms totally accessible to either sex, to any molester, gay, lesbian, bisexual or transgender person under the guise of "eliminating discrimination." The mayor models gay partnership with her same-sex lover while declaring the legislation is "the most personally meaningful thing I will ever do as mayor."

I wonder what "silent" ministers in the city will do when transgender men, identifying as women, walk in on their young daughters while they're using a public restroom?

Apostate ministers like Tony Campolo and Rob Bell are more up front in actually promoting the LGBT lifestyle through their so-called "biblically based" books, instructional DVDs, or their pulpit ministry. What message is sent to the youth of America when the minister at our National Cathedral in DC welcomes a transgender minister to preach with, "This is in support of greater equality for the transgender community... to send a message of love and affirmation especially to LGBT youth... that's the way God made you!"?

Here's the deal: People of faith must awaken to these demonic schemes to destroy marriage and family in America while not being surprised that more and more children and youth are entertaining demonically planted thoughts, such as "I'm gay" or "Am I gay?" We need godly counsel so we're prepared to handle this emergent reality.

My Child Says "I'm Gay": A Suggested Scriptural Strategy

1. *"Pray continually" (1 Thess. 5:17).* From the moment of the initial confession throughout the entire journey, pray and fast in faith the same way you would engage with God for someone's salvation or healing. *"With man this is impossible, but with God all things are possible" (Matt.19:26).* Reject all fatalism and leanings towards some predestination of your child to this lifestyle. Do not believe this to be a life sentence!

2. Listen lovingly and intentionally. *"Everyone should be quick to listen, slow to speak and slow to become angry..." (James 1:19).* Make a quality decision to keep

the lines of communication open from the initial disclosure and beyond. It will take time to process what's unfolding so avoid any knee-jerk response. "Pressure reveals the person," so draw on the grace of God to be gracious and self-controlled, remembering that youthful confusion about sexual identity is common.

Young people also are usually very uninformed about the serious health risks associated with the not-so-gay lifestyle. Counter the ignorance by sensitively sharing CDC facts—not made-up "scare tactics." In the final segment of our "Bullseye" journey we'll cover these realities.

3. Clarify exactly what your child means by "coming out as gay." *"The purposes of a man's heart are deep waters, but a man of understanding draws them out" (Prov. 20:5).* Is your son or daughter struggling with temptation towards the same sex or acting on the attraction? Is this an incident or a persistent pattern? If the openness is there (it's advisable to go dad with son/mom with daughter) gently go further to inquire about origins, fantasies, gay pornography, frequenting gay bars, and hanging with gay friends. Finally, try to ascertain what adult friends are influencing your son or daughter's thinking at this vulnerable and impressionable season of their life.

4. Encourage disclosure by calm and skillful inquiry. Ask if there has been sexual abuse, youthful curiosity and experimentation, adult manipulation or molestation, masturbation with gay pornography, etc. Lead the way here with humility, wisdom, and age-appropriate transparency regarding any of your youthful indiscretions (being discreet and avoiding names) and what lessons you learned.

5. In your prayerful preparation for times of discussion, avail yourself of the right resources. "Wolves in sheep's clothing" (Matt. 7:15) are out there like Matthew Vine,

Jay Bakker, Ray Boltz, and other gay-affirming leaders. They must be avoided like the plague! They're smooth and sneaky and seducing multitudes.

Instead go to the websites of Biblically faithful leaders like Dr. Michael Brown, Dr. David Foster, Dr. Robert Gagnon, Stephen Bennett, and, may I humbly submit, myself, for resources that will keep you on the right path and encourage you in your time of need. At the right time, may I suggest that you sit and watch together with your struggling son or daughter "Such Were Some of You" by David Foster's ministry or "Is Gay OK? 10 Things Everyone Needs to Know" at my website: larrytomczak.com. If your son or daughter is living at home under your authority, make this a directive, not an elective. Remember that you are not their "buddy" but their parent and one day you will give an account to God for their life.

6. *"Take your thoughts captive" (2 Cor. 10:5).* Knowing *"fear has torment" (1 Jn 4:17).* Be intentional in renouncing all negative thoughts such as "We'll never get through this... God is punishing us... What will our church think...? Our other children may follow... He'll bring his 'lover' over and neighbors will see... He'll die of AIDS... She'll kill herself." Be radical in replacing these destructive thoughts with faith-building thoughts as you wield the *"sword of the Spirit which is the word of God" (Eph. 6:17).* Go to larry-tomczak.com and listen regularly to "Biblical Declarations to Build Your Faith" as a free resource to keep you *"strong in the Lord and in the strength of His might" (Eph. 6:10).* In forty-four years of ministry, this has always been the number one requested resource!

7. Confide in trusted friends and, ideally, a pastor. *"Two are better than one, because they have a good return for their work: If one falls down, his friend can help him up" (Eccl. 4:9-10).* The Christian life was never intended to be lived in isolation but rather true community. Pray and

then approach those you trust so they can hold up your arms during this season.

8. Consider contacting "Lead Them Home Ministry" (leadthemhome.org) for supplemental help. This wonderful ministry trains church leaders and families how to minister to those with same-sex attraction. Their "Posture Shift" seminar and "Family Care" support team can come alongside of those in need until they find their breakthrough.

9. Extend compassion and care to your child without compromising or condoning the homosexual lifestyle. God requires absolute purity before marriage and total fidelity in marriage, as He ordained it, between one man and one woman. All sex outside of covenant marriage is sin, strictly prohibited, including ALL homosexual involvement.

When a child casually or flippantly says, "I'm coming out; I'm gay. I'm just affirming who I really am" a parent has a solemn responsibility to charitably and clearly set the standard straight. *"As for me and my house, we will serve the Lord" (Josh. 24:15).*

At God's appointed time, ideally the father, in a united front with the mother, must resist any manipulation or intimidation and state something like the following: "My son/daughter, we love you more than you can imagine and God allowed us as a couple to unite in a procreative act that brought you into this world. Your thinking is totally unacceptable to God and us. It dishonors our Lord Jesus Christ, who died on the cross to save us from our sins. It is contradictory to His eternal plan for marriage, which has been upheld for over 5000 years of Western civilization. Therefore this 'coming out' needs to be a coming out of deception and, like the prodigal son, returning to the God and Father who created you, loves you and has a wonderful destiny for your life. Have we made ourselves perfectly clear?"

10. Never forget your child is Jesus Christ's purchased possession whom He loves immensely and will fight to rescue from this deception. No matter what the culture conveys about the beauty and finality of homosexuality, it is built upon lies propagated by Satan himself. Only God knows how many hundreds of thousands of formerly deceived men and women have been set free from the bondage of this sinful and shameful lifestyle through the proclamation of the gospel and Biblical truth.

My Christian brother, Stephen Bennett, was entrapped in a lifestyle of depression, drugs, and homosexuality in which he gave himself to more than one hundred homosexual partners (many of whom are now dead from HIV/AIDS). He was born again in 1992. Today he lives a liberated life with his beautiful wife of over two decades and their two children. His full-time ministry is helping reach those identifying as LGBT (SBMinistries.org). What God has done for him and others, He can do for you!

"Don't you realize that this is not the way to live? Unjust people who don't care about God will not be joining in his kingdom. Those who use and abuse each other, use and abuse sex, use and abuse the earth and everything in it, don't qualify as citizens in God's kingdom. A number of you know from experience what I'm talking about, for not so long ago you were on that list. Since then you've been cleaned up and given a fresh start by Jesus, our Master, our Messiah, and by our God present in us, the Spirit." (1 Cor. 6:9-11 MSG).

Chapter 19
Gay Christians—Part I

Can A Christian Be Gay? (Part 1)
Departing a restaurant where we celebrated my wife's birthday recently, I got a 10 p.m. call on my cellphone. A lady in Kentucky needed help because her bank teller friend, who identifies as a Christian, was confused about homosexuality.

Her unmarried female friend read a book called *Torn: Rescuing the Gospel from the Gays-vs-Christians Debate* by Justin Lee, 36-year-old founder of the Gay Christian Network that "helps educate the Christian community about sexual issues from a biblical standpoint." Having feelings at times for members of the same sex, the woman's friend was being influenced by his theories and asking, "Is it OK to be a gay Christian?" "What about same-sex marriage?"

Lee encourages his followers to embrace counsel from the New Testament (Rom. 14) and "not quarrel over disputable matters" and choose one of two paths:

- Side A: God allows permanent, monogamous gay relationships.

- Side B: Gay Christians remain celibate.

As we continue our Bullseye Challenge, we'll devote the next four chapters to lesbian, gay, bisexual, and transgender (LGBT) issues. I strongly encourage you to take your time and study everything *carefully* in light of scripture, not pop culture or some so-called Christian leader manipulating God's unchanging Word. Be like the Berean believers who *"received the message with great eagerness and examined the Scriptures every day to see if what Paul said was true" (Acts 17:11).* These four chapters cover thoroughly and Biblically what is the most controversial and defining issue of this generation. Proceed with caution, an open mind, and an obedient heart. As Bono said in his song, "Mercy": "Love is charity and brings with it a clarity."

Here is part one. Go forward with humility and teachability to be greatly blessed.

I approach this subject not as an angry, mean-spirited extremist but rather in a spirit of humility, as a would-be friend of both supporters and opponents. As a Christian who was formerly a "rock star" drummer in a band called the Lost Souls (and I *was* lost!), I admit the church has unfortunately fallen far short in our testimony, due to divorce, hypocrisy, and uncharitable attitudes in our ranks. Yet I want to be part of the generation arising that is not so much imposing but proposing a better way that really does lead to peace, freedom, and long-term happiness in human relationships. I've engaged and befriended gays and regularly attended their gay-pride events for over a decade in different states. I've stood at the bedside of my buddy John who changed from gay to straight but later died of AIDS and requested I officiate his funeral (which I did, with his daughter and over 50 of his past gay friends present).

We're on a journey of discovery, and I hope this following counsel helps multitudes who are being asked similar questions as I'm asked.

Let's Not Be Non-Specific but Straightforward
The entire Bible unambiguously defines marriage between one man and one woman (Gen. 2:24 in the Old Testament; Matt. 19:5 in the Gospels; Eph. 5:31 in the New Testament). Outside that state, obedient Christians are called to sexual purity/celibacy (Eph. 5:3-6; Col. 3:5-6; 1 Cor. 6:9-11; 1 Thess. 4:3-8).

Paul says, "For the time will come when people will not put up with sound doctrine. Instead, to suit their own desires, they will gather around them a great number of teachers to say what their itching ears want to hear. They will turn their ears away from the truth and turn aside to myths" (2 Tim. 4:3-4 NIV).

Dr. Timothy Keller, world-renowned author and pastor, had to respond to similar inquiries at Oxford University. He lovingly and succinctly helped students with sound counsel from Scripture. He told them:

1. As Christians we're called to love, not disdain our neighbor—atheist, gay or antagonist.

2. If you call yourself gay and Christians disagree with you, that doesn't mean you're being judged unfairly.

3. 3The Bible clearly teaches that homosexuality is not God's way or design for His creation.

4. Don't let your sexuality destroy your objectivity (to come to grips with biblical truth).

5. Admittedly, some church people have attraction to the same sex but do not allow themselves to be governed by those feelings (temptations). Their identity in Christ is central, not their sexual identity. This shift is what frees them to both change and live changed.

6. God designed us for human intimacy—companionship, touch and sexual expression—in the right place and right time, but people can choose to fulfill normal desires in un-righteous ways. Key: it is a choice!

Not long ago, *Sex and the City* starlet Cynthia Nixon caused a firestorm when interviewed in a New York magazine saying that she did the heterosexual thing for a while but then chose to go gay.

Rosaria Butterfield, author of *The Secret Thoughts of an Unlikely Convert*, describes how she was a leftist lesbian professor who "despised Christians then somehow became one!" Now she's married to a pastor, raising her children in North Carolina.

A friend of mine was a lesbian for forty-two years until she found freedom after being "born again" as a Christian. She's been free from the lifestyle for over twenty years!

Understanding the Bible Correctly

Today, there's a lot of misunderstanding regarding Scripture because some gay-affirming leaders and churches take a "salad bar" approach, conveniently selecting passages that support positions while neglecting other, more challenging ones.

Some people are dishonest with Scriptures (intentionally or unintentionally): "Where in the Bible does it even mention cocaine or pornography?" "I haven't seen gay marriage in the Bible once!" (This actually came from a chairman of one of our political parties.)

Others "cherry pick" verses to defend conduct without taking into consideration the context or the whole of what Scripture teaches on a topic ("A text out of context is a pretext."). The fact is, the Good Book doesn't categorically say, "Don't judge"; "Don't dance"; "Don't drink"; "Don't enjoy sex"; or dozens of other so-called "prohibitions" many erroneously believe. Neither does it tell us in *every* situation to "turn the other cheek"; "hand over our cloak"; "give and expect no return"; or scores of other recommendations that need to be clearly explained in their context.

Sometimes people try to discredit the Bible by mocking its content and citing Old Testament passages that seem outdated or severe in application. What they don't understand is this: there are basically three types of laws prominent in the Old Testament/Hebrew Bible: 1) ceremonial, 2) hygienic and 3) moral.

The first two (ceremonial and hygienic) don't apply anymore for those who are part of the New Covenant since the time of Christ; otherwise there would be no more football (handling a pig skin was a no-no), and the over-forty crowd couldn't approach the altar of God nor those with a disability or during that "time of the month." ("You mean I can go get a Wendy's cheeseburger with bacon, have some Red Lobster jumbo shrimp, or enjoy a HoneyBaked Ham?" Absolutely!) Yet the moral laws do still apply—not for or as a means to redemption but to show us our need to be redeemed!

It really is time to gain a better understanding of the Bible, not primarily as a harsh legalistic code of dos and don'ts but rather as a guidebook of timeless wisdom. It also provides us with a coherent framework for outlining society's problems, then prescribes answers to remedy them.

Our challenge is simple: Will we follow a secular or a scriptural worldview? I suggest we embrace our Creator's ways for His creation. "For best results, follow instructions in the manufacturer's handbook!"

Ten Reasons Why Practicing Homosexuals Can't Be Christians
Multitudes today are confused about gay-related issues. It's easier to "go with the flow" and steer clear of the intimidation to conform. The PC (politically correct) police are ever present.

Because few of us want to be perceived as "backward and bigoted homophobes" (as tolerance advocates often brand those with whom they disagree) or as people who are not in step with the "progressive, equality, non-judgmental" mantra, it's easy to clam up and play it cool, saying things like, "Of course I'm for equality and non-discrimination." But that's not an option for faithful, obedient followers of Jesus! As Dr. Martin Luther King Jr. warned, "When we learn the truth but choose to remain silent, that's when we begin to die."

Dr. Alveda King, Martin's niece, told me in an interview for our video project *Is Gay OK? 10 Things Every Christian Needs to Know*, that if her uncle were alive today, he would remain steadfast in defense of Biblical marriage and reject attempts to justify immoral conduct as a "civil right." He'd remind us again of his oft-quoted words concerning the church's role in society: "The church is neither the master of the state nor the servant of the state, but rather the conscience of the state."

1. To call oneself an authentic Christian and remain a practicing homosexual is a direct contradiction of Biblical teaching and contrary to the "abundant life" promised by Jesus.

   Just as "Christian hatred" is an oxymoron, so too is the term "gay Christian." God offers forgiveness and freedom through His Son, which is the good news (gospel) of the Christian message.

   According to the Christian faith, once a person responds to the gospel message in repentance and faith, he or she finds a new start to then fulfill their destiny in life.

Even as Saul of Tarsus, a murderer, became Paul the apostle, a great saint and missionary leader, Christianity asserts that God redeems repentant people who may be "homosexuals, adulterers, drunkards, idolaters or whatever" and transforms their lives! It happened in the "San Francisco" of their day—Corinth—and has been repeated all over the world. Jesus Christ didn't invade human history as the world's Messiah to merely make our selfish, sinful lives a little better and more prosperous. He came to totally transform our lives and not only forgive our sins but free us from sin's power!

2. Practicing homosexuality is most definitely sinful and contradicting Biblical teaching on God's order for human relationships and family.

Simply stated, there is *not* one single verse in the entire Bible condoning homosexual activity. On the contrary, it is strongly prohibited throughout the Old and New Testaments.

We're aware that this is contrary to what some "religious," "gay-affirming" churches and leaders put forth (they reject the authority of the Bible and twist the meaning of passages), but they must be challenged and called back to faithfulness to the truth.

The Bible consistently, unambiguously, and without exception prohibits practicing homosexuality and tells us to honor God's design for sexual behavior between men and women. The purpose is that we enjoy a fulfilling sexual experience in marriage and ideally have children as an expression of our marital love. Stating this forthrightly is not "hate speech." This is an expression of divine love because sinful behavior not only hurts our Creator, but also is harmful to us (and others). God gives us laws for our own good!

3. Homosexuality is not simply another "alternative lifestyle." In the Hebrew-Christian Bible, there are multiple times in both the Old and New Testament accounts when homosexuality and other immoral activities are

explicitly condemned as dishonorable to God and the natural order (the way things were designed to work) and as destructive to those involved with them. An entire chapter in the Old Testament lists certain activities and calls them "detestable," stating in no uncertain terms, "Stay away!" The New Testament uses five terms to describe both male and female homosexual conduct: "unnatural," "perverted," "degrading," "shameful," and "indecent." Not to be facetious, but is that hard to understand? Scripture throughout forbids us to be sexually involved in seven areas: with parents, with children, with brothers and sisters, with another's spouse, with animals, with dead people, and with the same sex. These never change.

4. All of us are born with a fallen nature that gives us a tendency to do wrong.

We don't have to train children to lie, steal, harm others, act selfishly, or demand their own way. Having a free will to make choices, all of us are accountable for our own actions. Biology can't make us do wrong, although circumstances can influence us. To say otherwise leaves people as victims, not responsible for their behavior—a convenient excuse. That's like what a present-day celebrity, married eight years with two sons, who shamelessly committed adultery with a younger country singer and then left his wife to marry her, did. He later told his wife, "It wasn't your fault. I've cheated from day one. It's just who I am."

According to Scripture and science, homosexuality has never been proven to be part of someone's biological constitution, so everyone decides his or her lot in life (although all of us are influenced differently). The bottom line: we do express understanding regarding people's upbringing while not releasing people from taking personal responsibility for their actions.

Chapter 20
Gay Christians—Part II

There is a major distinction between people's behavior and their race.

My black friends can't decide to become Caucasian. My wife can't decide to become a full-blown man (though today some try!). One is chosen; the other is not chosen. Homosexuality is something someone does, not something someone is. Each of us is personally responsible for our behavior. (Otherwise, drunk drivers, rapists, and child molesters are "off the hook" and play the "victim card.") To confuse this wrongly creates a new "minority" status and special "rights" for a very small segment of the population representing no more than two to three percent (not the inaccurate, inflated figures of ten percent or more).

Note: Even this two to three percent may be less because some cite a prison experience, college experimentation or one-time, drug-influenced encounter as part of "homosexual" background.

The cause of homosexuality is complex, yet there are common, agreed-upon contributing factors:

- The person's self-will

- A dysfunctional home environment

- Spousal or child abuse

- Seduction by peers or authority figures. (Studies show that approximately eighty-five percent of

lesbians were abused or molested and forty percent
of gay men were seduced or molested by older gay
men when they were young boys.)

• Media influence

• Pornography

• Drugs

• Absence of a father

• Childhood experience/experimentation

• Confusion about identity/misunderstanding "artistic
  bent"

Some people are definitely more susceptible to homosexuality than
others (proclivity vs. practice).

Some individuals are "wired" more toward these artistic areas:
music, singing, dance, poetry, cooking, clothing design, hairstyling,
and painting as opposed to football, baseball, basketball, hunting,
wrestling, and other athletics. These differences are healthy and
make for diversity in the human family. Yet if a dad who enjoys
contact sports ridicules a son who doesn't, or if a parent doesn't
affirm a daughter's femininity, a child can feel misunderstood and
rejected and very vulnerable to outside, negative influences.

One of my sons was more athletic, the other more artistic. I tried to
affirm their individual bents with unconditional love, while helping
both develop their masculinity. Today my older son is married with
three children and is a type-A leader running aggressive political
campaigns. My younger son has been married for over a decade, has
two sons, and is the pastor of a thriving church.

There is a difference between desire and deed.

Many good people lie in their beds wrestling with feelings and
fantasies regarding homosexuality. Just because someone is tempted
in an area does not mean they are guilty of sexual misconduct. As
they say, "You can't stop birds flying around your head, but you can
stop them from building a nest in your hair!"

Also, just because someone has homosexual desires and states
they don't "feel" there's anything wrong with acting upon them, that
doesn't make it right. Objective standards, not subjective feelings,

have to govern our lives, or else people can justify all kinds of behavior—such as pedophilia, rape, or child molestation.

The Brown University student health plan is now going to cover sex changes (called "gender reassignment") if a girl wants to morph into a male or vice versa! Scriptural standards, not experience or feelings, must be our guide, or the moral confusion will only get worse.

God loves all people, and it is His plan to see us change to fulfill our destiny.

Jesus Christ welcomed and accepted everyone but called them to change unrighteous lifestyles: the adulteress, the multi-lover Samaritan, the corrupt tax collectors. He said, "Go and sin no more!" And when they obeyed, they discovered the same life of freedom, peace, and joy available to us today!

Homosexual behavior can be changed, as evidenced by multitudes throughout America and in the Bible.

I personally know a woman who left a lesbian lifestyle after forty-two years and several male former homosexuals who today are happily married with numerous children. Organizations helping homosexuals find freedom through compassionate counseling are filled with the testimonies of thousands of real people who really have changed. Consider also high-profile celebrities who've done likewise:

- Actress Anne Heche left her homosexual partnership with Ellen DeGeneres to marry a man, as did singer Sinead O'Connor when she married Nick Sommerlad.

- Three-time MVP in the WNBA and two-time gold medalist Sheryl Swoopes actually did it in reverse! She was married with an eight-year-old when she decided to divorce her husband for her "lover," Alisa Scott.

Going from "straight to gay" or "gay to straight" undermines the theory that sexual orientation is inherited and unchangeable. You might call this "inconvenient truth." Some states have even passed a law forbidding anyone to counsel anyone until age eighteen that change is possible!

In light of all we've examined, it should be clear to anyone who calls, writes, or asks about the issues we've discussed that there really are answers to the legitimate questions being asked. Maybe the reader believed some of the myths and misinformation circulating in our culture, believing them to be fact. But as John Keynes, the British economist who influenced the economic policies of many governments, used to say, "When facts change, I change my mind! What do you do?"

Chapter 21
Transgenderism

Testimony of a Transformed Transgender Person by Linda Seiler
The world applauded as Bruce Jenner announced his transition to Caitlyn. However, I couldn't join the celebration. People may judge me for being intolerant, but the truth is, I understand Bruce's anguish in a way that most people don't, for I also come from a transgender background.

From my earliest memory, I felt like a boy trapped in a girl's body. It wasn't a fleeting thought or a phase; it was an obsession to have male genitalia, and it dominated my life for decades. My parents had no idea I was dealing with transgender issues. They thought I was just a tomboy and that I would eventually outgrow that phase.

At age nine, I heard about sex-change operations, and I concluded that that was the answer to my dilemma. I devised a plan: as soon as I was old enough and had enough money, I would change my name to David, have a sex change, and live happily ever after.

In sixth grade, when all the other girls were experimenting with makeup and wanting to date boys, I wanted nothing to do with that. I hated my body and the fact that it was beginning to show signs of femininity. I was deeply jealous of the boys around me whose voices were changing, and I desperately wanted that for myself. I became depressed and suicidal. Around the same time, I discovered, to my

horror, that I was attracted to women instead of men. (I realize that
not all transgendered persons have same-sex attractions, but I did.) I
didn't want those attractions—I desperately wanted to fit in with the
other kids who were naturally attracted to the opposite sex. And yet,
it made sense that if I was a heterosexual man trapped in a woman's
body that I should be attracted to women. I just needed to hold out
long enough until I could get the sex change.

In late junior high, I starting thinking through the ramifications
of my decisions in a way I hadn't when I was nine years old. No one
knew my secret, and I was too ashamed to tell anyone. I feared how
my family would respond if I had a sex change. Would they reject
me? What would the neighbors think? What if I lost everything? I
concluded that I had two options. I could run away, have the sex
change, and never see my family again. Or, I could forego the
operation—which would mean a continued life of loneliness and
suicidal despair—but at least I'd still have my family. I chose the
latter and decided from that point forward that I had better try to
look more like a girl so no one would ever know my secret.

It became increasingly difficult not to act on my attractions in
high school. I thought that perhaps dating boys and experimenting
sexually with them would "awaken" something in me that had been
dormant. But all it did was intensify my jealousy—I wanted to be
the man with a woman.

I became a Christian during my junior year in high school and
thought that when I woke up the next morning that all my desires
would go away. When they didn't, I realized I was in a dilemma,
as I discovered the Church was not a safe place to deal with such
issues. I lived a double life, appearing to be a Christian who had it all
together on the outside. But behind closed doors, I was an absolute
sex addict, enslaved to compulsive masturbation and pornography,
driven by a sexual fetish involving urinals, and emotionally
enmeshed with every woman who invested in me.

During my senior year in college, I couldn't take it anymore and
confessed to my campus pastor. He responded with compassion,
noting the courage it must have taken to share the secret I had
harbored for over twenty-one years. He said that my confession
didn't change his opinion of me and that he was committed to getting
me the help I needed. I'm so glad he demonstrated compassion

without compromising the truth. That was the beginning of what was to be an eleven-year journey of transformation.

The healing process wasn't easy. I would be full of faith one day and down in the dumps the next. Well-meaning Christian counselors told me that my issues were not something that could be resolved and that they could only help me "cope" on this side of heaven until I experienced ultimate freedom upon death. But the Lord lodged a seed of faith in my spirit that nothing is impossible for Him. By His grace, I determined to hold fast to the hem of Jesus' garment until I experienced the freedom He died to give me—no matter how long it took or how difficult the journey.

The transformation journey involved redemptive relationships with sisters in Christ who were not threatened by my attractions and who affirmed me as a woman among women. I also benefitted from brothers in Christ who affirmed me as a sister. Over time, I began to realize that my desire to bond with attractive, spiritual women was nothing more than an attempt to complete my own femininity, which I saw lacking in myself. I had never identified with my own gender due to emotional wounds from childhood. I honestly believed it was inferior to be a woman and that only males were made in the image of God—Eve was just an afterthought created to meet all of Adam's needs. Women were second-class citizens.

Through in-depth counseling and Spirit-led emotional healing prayer, Jesus spoke to my deepest wounds, replaced lies with His truth, and showed me the value of being a woman made in God's image. In addition, I forgave those who rejected me and reinforced the lie that it was not good to be the girl God created me to be. Although I saw myself as a victim, the Lord showed me that I also had to repent for my own wrong responses to those who had rejected me. As a result of confessing my sin in the light, forgiving those who had hurt me, and repenting of my own wrong reactions, the enemy lost the legal ground he had to hold me in bondage. I was free to experience the nurturing, compassionate love of God in a way that satisfied the deep thirst in my feminine soul. The end result was that I no longer wanted to be a man and no longer found myself attracted to women because Jesus had satisfied the deepest longings of my heart. As my healing continued to play out in the ensuing years, attractions to men began to surface. It was thrilling, yet awkward, going through emotional puberty in my mid-thirties!

Again, the journey wasn't easy. In fact, it was messy. It took great patience on the part of those who walked alongside me when, at times, it seemed hopeless that I would ever change.

But don't believe the lie that transformation isn't possible. Today, I am a heterosexual woman, content in my own body and exclusively attracted to men. It didn't happen overnight—it was a grueling, eleven-year journey—but it did happen. And the journey was well worth it. Now I'm living the dream I never thought was possible. I'm living as my true self, as the woman God created me to be.

Some claim that offering hope for change is detrimental and will drive people to the brink of suicide. For me, it was quite the opposite. Jesus set me free from decades of suicidal depression! I had fantasized about becoming a man; I had hoped I would find completion in the arms of another woman. But that all left me empty and thirsting for more. Nothing in this world could fill my emptiness and alleviate my anguish. Only Jesus could hold my heart and heal the deepest part of my being.

While I disagree with Bruce Jenner's opinion that transitioning will resolve all his issues, I understand why he chose that path. Had my circumstances been different, I would have done the same thing. However, there's no scalpel that cuts deep enough to heal the heart. You can rearrange the skin on the outside, but it doesn't rearrange your past and the emotional anguish you suffer as a result. Those will still be there after the outer wounds heal. That's why the suicide rate for post-operative transsexuals is so high. In fact, Johns Hopkins hospital stopped performing sex-reassignment surgeries because follow-up studies indicated that surgery did not relieve their patients' mental anguish.[1] The emotional wounds that drive someone toward sex reassignment are real, yet I know firsthand that they can find true and lasting resolve in the compassionate, healing love of Jesus.

Transformation without physical surgery is possible—through emotional heart surgery. Not everyone wants it, and Jesus won't

---

[1] See http://www.wsj.com/articles/paul-mchugh-transgender-surgery-isnt-the-solution-1402615120

force it on anyone; he respects your free will. But if you know someone who struggles with these issues and is looking for hope, I want them to know there are other voices out there besides those who advocate the path that Bruce/Caitlyn Jenner has taken.

I encourage you to watch the three-minute video of my story of transformation, and visit www.suchweresomeofyou.org for even more stories like mine.

Chapter 22
Homosexuality and Boy Scouts

Will You Endanger Your Son Through Boy-Scout Involvement in Days Ahead?

"A nation that prefers disgrace to danger is prepared for a master and deserves one."

—*Alexander Hamilton*

In the middle of the Cold War, then-Governor Ronald Reagan quoted the above warning in his 1964 classic speech, "A Time to Choose." Similar to Winston Churchill awakening Great Britain amidst the growing Nazi threat in 1940, the "Great Communicator" sensed a gathering storm and challenged multitudes capitulating to big-government socialism and communism.

For eight years, I've served with other courageous leaders investing a significant portion of ministry to compassionately confront the dangerous acceptance of sexual behavior that the Bible labels as "moral impurity", "degrading", "shameless", "indecent", "unnatural" and "perversion" (Rom. 1:24-27). While we are to reach out in love to every individual, we must resist an agenda dishonoring our Creator, undermining the sanctity of marriage and attempting to redefine it so homosexual unions, polyamory, and polygamy are considered acceptable, normal, and beautiful.

LGBTQ activism hit us at warp speed. Many leaders, charged with the responsibility to equip and protect the flock, have dismissed this as negativism and non-urgent. Others listened politely but wanted to avoid controversy, which offends church members and affects giving. Some recognized the seismic shift in our culture and were jolted out of passivity to prayerful activism. Now we must all awaken to "smell the coffee" and recognize silence is not an option in light of the avalanche crashing upon us.

With the Supreme Court's ruling on gay marriage (bear in mind that there is a higher authority—Almighty God) and conservative, Catholic Ireland approving homosexual marriage by popular vote, we now face the president of the Boy Scouts of America basically calling for an overhaul of the 105-year-old organization's mission in order to include homosexual troop leaders! Adding this to the nonstop attack on our religious freedoms and the chilling scenario of what lies ahead, may people and pastors across America finally stand up before it's too late. BSA President Robert Gates recently declared, "We must deal with the world as it is, not as we might wish it to be. The status quo in our movement's membership standards cannot be sustained."

The homosexual advocacy group "Scouts for Equality" hailed it as "another step forward!" Undiscerning onlookers applauded it as enlightenment, equality, political correctness, tolerance, sexual diversity, and gender-neutral advancement. "This will open the door for transgenders just like in the Girl Scouts!" came the congratulatory cheer.

Mr. Gates, who previously homosexualized our United States military as a proponent for repealing "Don't Ask Don't Tell," now makes those upholding the Boy Scout Oath and the value of moral strength a human piñata. Engage in sodomy—you're progressive; uphold Christian standards—you're prejudiced and part of the problem.

The Boy Scout Oath and Past Leadership Examples
"On my honor I will do my best to do my duty to God and my country and to obey the Scout Law; to help other people at all times; to keep myself physically strong, mentally awake and *morally straight*" (emphasis mine).

Honoring chastity until married; upholding fidelity to one's spouse; avoiding homosexuality and steering clear of pornography are all encompassed in the commitment to remain morally straight, along with a commitment to patriotism, courage, loyalty, integrity, and service. For decades it has been referred to living a "clean life," not what revisionists now reinterpret as living "honestly"— being true to who you really are whether gay, straight, bisexual, transgender, or whatever!

The Christian British military officer who founded scouting in 1910, Robert Baden-Powell, was a man of exemplary integrity. Later he commissioned an American, William Boyce, to launch the Boy Scouts in America, aligning them with the Young Men's Christian Association for meetings. To this day, the overwhelming majority of Boy Scouts gather in Christian churches and Mormon facilities across the USA.

Scouting changed slightly over the decades yet character development has always been at its core. "Try and leave this world a little better than you found it" were Baden-Powell's final words to Scouts prior to his death.

Do you recall reading the inspirational, character-building publication of the Boy Scouts, "Boys' Life," which debuted with a Norman Rockwell cover? Were you one of the 110 million boys who found their lives positively transformed through the Boy Scouts since its inception?

Do you recall the famous Boy Scouts put forth as models for us to emulate over the years?

Here are just a few: Dr. Martin Luther King Jr., Neil Armstrong, Andy Griffith, Hank Aaron, John Wayne, Sam Walton, Walter Cronkite, Jimmy Stewart, Gerald Ford, John F. Kennedy, George W. Bush, J.W. Marriott Jr., and Bill Gates. What did they all have in common? These were men who, though not flawless, demonstrated manliness and inspired us to become masculine leaders in our personal lives and future families.

Future Scenario?

Over the past few years, Boy Scout chapters have battled incessant bullying. A handful of homosexual-leaning Scouts initiated lawsuits; some local officials forced them out of public facilities; gay activists have pressured corporations to withhold funding until BSA changed its policy; and, high-profile politicians and celebrities made disparaging remarks about this wonderful organization being homophobic and bigoted. And since there has been so much silence from the faith-based community, the LGBTQ activists have had a field day!

There is also gross ignorance when it comes to homosexuality in our nation. The latest Gallup poll shows that the majority of citizens believe that twenty-four percent of Americans are either gay or lesbian! The real number is somewhere between two and three percent. And even that may be high because many confused people identify this way having experimented with the lifestyle in college or in prison, even though there's no further involvement today.

For the record, Boy Scouts are not discriminating by upholding standards for leadership and looking out for young impressionable boys. In 2000, the United States Supreme Court ruled that Boy Scouts had the absolute right, under well-established constitutional rights to free speech and free association, to refuse "to promote homosexual conduct as a legitimate form of behavior" (Dale v. Boy Scouts of America). Just as a men's softball league excludes females and a women's yoga exercise club isn't open to men, this is simply associational freedom as a constitutional right.

The Boy Scout oath calls our sons to do their "duty to God" and remain "morally straight." No major world religion sanctions homosexual marriage, even though some dissident, sectarian groups rebel against their religion's tenets, which have existed for thousands of years!

Picture leaving a Boy Scouts gathering at your church when a homosexual troop leader is seen crossing the parking lot, holding hands with his male lover. Before entering the car they exchange a sensual kiss. Your young son stops abruptly, looks at you, confused and saddened, then lays it on the line like kids do.

"Mom, why are those two men holding hands and kissing each other? My friend Joe told me that our troop leader is 'married' to another man. That's gross! I feel weird when I'm around him. Do I have to go on our camping trip? What if I find myself alone with him even if only for a few minutes? I don't like that."

Or what if you start noticing changes in your son since his involvement with the new gay Scout leader? Young boys are very susceptible to imitating authority figures and guys they think are cool. For those who disagree, just study the research or go to your nearest movie theater and watch young boys imitating Ironman, Spiderman, or the other action heroes they want to be like. When I was in elementary school I tried to imitate my gym teacher, Mr. B. He was a bodybuilder and a cop and I imitated his mannerisms and speech. I did the same with Rocky Colavito, my baseball hero. A few years later I joined millions of young people trying to emulate the Beatles, even forming a rock group with my buddies called the Lost Souls, after the Beatles appeared on a television variety show. Let's get real about this! Imitation is the most sincere form of flattery.

Finally, this one is the elephant in the room but let's hit it straight on: pedophilia. In a study published by the Archives of Sexual Behavior (not a Christian organization or a conservative research group), research revealed that "86 percent of offenders against males describe themselves as homosexual or bisexual." Likewise, the Family Research Council states unequivocally that "since almost 30% of child sexual abuse is committed by homosexual or bisexual men but less than 3% of American men identify themselves as homosexual or bisexual, we can infer that homosexual or bisexual men are approximately ten times more likely to molest children than heterosexual men."

I cried when I was a boy because I could not become a Boy Scout. We were poor and had no automobile; my dad was a maintenance man and my mother scrubbed floors three days a week. At the time their inability to serve in some capacity ruled me out and it broke my heart.

If the Boy Scouts of America caves to propaganda and pressure and buys into the misguided persuasion of Mr. Gates, my heart will break again.

When the New York Times ran an op-ed by Kathy Tisdale, leader of Camp Fire USA, heralding their "nondiscrimination policy" as contrasted with BSA, she stated something that can encourage us in closing. She challenged "those whose values or religious convictions may conflict with our policy to choose another organization to join."

Are you familiar with Trail Life USA, the Christian Boy Scout alternative that is growing rapidly throughout America and is based on uncompromising Biblical values?

And with the Girl Scouts of America welcoming transgender boy/girls into their ranks, where boy/girls can enter young girls' dressing rooms, restrooms, and exercise rooms, is it any wonder that American Heritage Girls, a Christian alternative, is exploding across America, with over 40,000 girls involved? Based on timeless, Biblical values, they declare that they're "not about girl power but God's power!"

Dads and Moms, Granddads and Grandmas, and hopefully a swelling rank of pastors, can I get an Amen to that?

Chapter 23
Understanding Social Justice

Racism, Fatherlessness, Sex Trafficking, Climate Change, Income Inequality, and Poverty
In the Old Testament God decrees: *"He has shown you O man what is good, and what does the Lord require of you? To do justice and to love mercy and to walk humbly with your God" (Mic. 6:8).*

In the New Testament He declares, *"True religion is this: to care for orphans and widows in their distress and to keep oneself from being stained by the world" (Jas 1:27).*

The above Biblical passages underscore the centrality of justice and concern for those who are less fortunate. In this last section of our Bullseye Challenge we want to examine some areas that are often neglected but are essential for Christians who want to live authentically and make a difference as agents of change in this world.

You don't want to run the risk of growing old dreaming of what could have been. Your biography is being written one day at a time. At the end of the age, you don't want to be bored reading your own life story when it could have been an adventure novel. God has called you to live adventurously and help make this world a better place.

Helen Keller, blind and deaf from the age of two, refused to be overcome by her disability. Rather than retreating into the darkness of her world, she passionately pursued the dreams God gave her. "Security is mostly a superstition. It does not exist in nature, nor do the children of men as a whole experience it," she commented. "Avoiding danger is no safer in the long run then outright exposure. Life is either a daring adventure, or nothing."

Some people shrink back, wondering what would happen if they fail when they step out in some area to make a difference in the world.

Let me make this crystal-clear: God is more pleased when you step out and make mistakes than when you sit back and do nothing for fear of failure. You cannot please God when you try to avoid making mistakes. Best of all, God is more than able to redeem your mistakes!

As we are becoming informed influencers in our generation and unafraid to speak up charitably and courageously on the major issues of our day, we will advance God's agenda for social justice in our generation. Notice that I said "God's agenda" for there are many human agendas in this sphere that do not align with God's will.

Only one question remains. Are you a candidate to join the ranks of spiritual pioneers who with reckless abandon join God's army to be a catalyst for change in this world? Will you become a part of the righteous revolution being formed in our day?

The Call for a Righteous Revolution

"Maly! Maly!" The crowd chanted that Christmas Eve night in 1989.

Vaclav Maly, a defrocked Catholic priest, had become the focal point of Czechoslovakia's "Velvet Revolution."

Since 1981, the communist government had assigned Maly to clean toilets in the Prague subway system for preaching the gospel. But eight years later, as the communist regime began crumbling, the people turned to the man who introduced them to freedom.

The incessant calls of "Maly, Maly!" by 800,000 people crowded onto the streets beckoned this bold believer from the belly of the subway system. As he emerged, he led the throng into the Old Town Square and then conducted an impromptu church service, offering forgiveness to his communist former captors. By the hundreds, people answered his call to come forward and repent for their past and to begin a new future.

And that is how Czechoslovakia's revolution took place. No bloodshed. No violence.

Vaclav Havel, the formerly imprisoned poet who became president, met with Maly and offered him the kingdom. "Father Maly, you can be anything you want in this government, from prime minister on down!"

"Oh no!" Maly replied. "I just want to preach the gospel. I just want to tell people about Jesus." Then he returned to his church. He, like us, knew that transformation in society begins with transformation in the human heart through the gospel of Jesus Christ.

Today there is the smell of a righteous revolution in the air—a revolution led by courageous Christians in the faith of this above hero. Governments may not be overthrown, but hearts will be transformed as men and women answer God's call to declare and demonstrate authentic Christianity. Together we follow a revolutionary leader, share a revolutionary message, and live a revolutionary lifestyle.

God is Looking for Heroes
King David spoke for God when he declared, *"I will make the godly of the land my heroes" (Ps. 101:6 TLB).* We may not win a Heisman Trophy, an Olympic Gold Medal, a Nobel Peace Prize or Congressional Medal of Honor, but we can surrender our lives to Jesus Christ and let him use us as agents of change, making a significant impact on the world around us. Our lifestyle should be so courageous in the cause of Christ that it demands an explanation!

In this dark hour of our nation's history, what will our peers, children, and grandchildren say about us? Because of our nearly month-long investment in this challenge, may they be inspired as we understand the critical issues of our time and speak the truth uncompromisingly from God's perspective.

Yes, let it be said of us, like Winston Churchill said of the courageous Royal Air Force pilots who rose to save Great Britain from destruction and Hitler in World War II, "Never was so much owed by so many to so few." Remember, a hero and a coward are both scared, but a hero runs in the right direction!

Erwin Lutzer, in his book *When a Nation Forgets God*, cited a German eyewitness in the 1940s who was part of a church flanked by railroad tracks. He wrote the following.

We heard stories of what was happening to the Jews, but we tried to distance ourselves from it because we felt, what could anyone do to stop it? Each Sunday morning, we would hear the train whistle blowing in the distance, then the wheels coming over the tracks. We became disturbed when we heard cries coming from the train is it passed by. We realized it was carrying Jews like cattle in cars!

Week after week the whistle would blow. We dreaded to hear the sounds of those wheels because we knew that we would hear the cries of the Jews in route to the death camp. Their screams tormented us. We also knew the time the train was coming and when we heard the whistle blow, we began singing hymns. By the time the train came past our church, we were singing at the top of our voices. If we heard the screams, we sang even more loudly and soon we heard them no more.

Years have passed and no one talks about it now, but I still hear the train whistle in my sleep.

In our time, there are the silent screams of 57 million unborn babies who lost their lives through abortion on demand. Unscrupulous companies pretend they're caring for women when actually they're terminating lives of future women and deriving riches from the abortion industry. There are people exploited and kidnapped in sex trafficking. There are immigrants who want a better life and want to do things righteously but they're being hindered through greedy individuals standing in their way. Orphans long for a father and a mother. Sick and dying people lack proper medical care and need a helping hand. People die prematurely and suffer debilitating diseases because individuals refuse to care for the environment in proper ways. Poverty abounds and multitudes are shackled in its vise-like grip. Phony politicians pontificate about programs and how much they care when behind the scenes they're accumulating

enormous sums of money unscrupulously, while their annual
financial disclosures reveal a paltry pittance given to alleviate
poverty in our day.

There are so many other areas that come under the heading of
social justice but let's start here. Since time and space do not permit
us to be as comprehensive as we'd like, let's make a few closing
points before we pursue a more in-depth analysis of some critical
areas.

- Climate change and environmental concerns will be
  debated *ad infinitum* but as Christians we are com-
  pelled to be good stewards of God's resources and
  earth. We can make a quality decision to reasonably
  conserve energy and avoid waste. Water is precious
  and should be conserved; the same is true with food
  when millions starve weekly.

- Justice for orphans requires individuals to prayerfully consider adoption or financially supporting
  those pursuing it. We adopted a Korean child. My
  son adopted Nicaraguan and South African boys. My
  other son married a single mom with two small children. It costs close to $40,000 for most adoptions.
  All of us should do our part through prayer and financial investment to assist the fatherless in finding
  homes.

- Racism must be eradicated and each one of us should
  be an extension of God's love to all peoples on the
  earth. We can renounce prideful attitudes of superi-
  ority towards those who are different from us and
  steer clear of all cruel ethnic joking and stereotyping.
  Building bridges and serving in our communities
  with others of different ethnic origin honors God.
  Leaders in our churches must be proactive to deseg-
  regate and then populate God's family to reflect the
  rainbow colors He designed. Our former church was
  forty percent black because of intentionality demonstrated by leadership.

• Jesus told us, *"The poor you will always have with you."* No one is going to totally eliminate poverty but we can all do our part by sacrificial giving and practical serving. Generous giving and volunteering in churches with initiatives to help the underprivileged; financially supporting reputable relief agencies like Samaritans Purse or World Vision; going on mission trips to help build homes, schools, and hospitals in Third World countries; and volunteering in city missions and soup kitchens are simply a few outlets wherein we can take care of these whom Jesus called "the least of these my brethren."

At this point I will take a moment to encourage us to be discerning regarding politicians exploiting the issue of poverty to manipulate people for votes. They'll cry "Income inequality!" and stoke the fires of discontentment, while promising incredible entitlements to those who will put them in office. Many of these ambitious office-seekers are very rich and try to project an image of compassion and cover up their unscrupulous conduct behind the scenes. They're also willing to mortgage our children's future by obscene spending of our tax money to pay for their irresponsible ways.

As we come down the home stretch in our Bullseye Challenge, let's reflect on the profound reminder Jesus gave us in this realm of social justice.

"When the Son of Man comes in His glory, and all the angels with him, He will sit on His throne in heavenly glory. All the nations will be gathered before Him and He will separate the people one from another as a shepherd separates the sheep from the goats" (Matt. 25:31-32).

Salvation comes by grace through faith, not by good works (Eph. 2:8-9), yet the reality of one's salvation is proved by a person's works. Remember this as you read on of Jesus promising a wonderful inheritance and heavenly home for those who heed these words:

"I was hungry and you gave me something to eat. I was thirsty and you gave me something to drink. I was a stranger and you invited me in. I needed clothes and you clothed me. I was sick and you looked after me. I was in prison and you came to visit me... I tell you the truth, whatever you did for one of the least of these my brethren, you did it for Me" (Matt. 25:35-36; 40).

Chapter 24
Abortion

Responses to the 10 Most Common Pro-choice Arguments
Grab a seat. This one is hard to believe.

Many newspapers across our country feature a weekly human-interest story about newlyweds and how they found love. *The New York Times* is no different with their "Vows" section.

Recently Udonis Haslem, NBA star for the Miami Heat, and his new wife, Faith Rein, were given their moment in the spotlight. The "college sweethearts" part was endearing—but hold on to your hat as they share something unique.

"Their first challenge took place the following spring when she became pregnant," the article says. "It was her junior and his senior year, and he had begun training for the NBA draft. Despite the pregnancy, she was busy with track meets and helping him complete homework. The timing was bad."

"I am not a huge fan of abortion, but we both had sports careers, plus we could not financially handle a baby," the paper quotes Haslem as saying.

"Udonis appreciated that I was willing to have an abortion," Rein then says. "I found him caring, supportive, and nurturing and all over me to be sure I was OK. I saw another side of him during that difficult time and fell deeply in love. He had a big heart and was the whole package."

Come again? Will this be the wave of the future for wedding announcements if we don't experience a true awakening in America? This is why I am so passionate about equipping believers to better engage lost people and people who are deceived regarding the sanctity of life issue in our culture. I invite you to join me as authentic salt-and-light Christians.

Pro-abortion websites and publications are not remaining silent. They are excited about this kind of development in the world's most prominent newspaper and are doing their part to equip people on the other side.

The Frisky lauded it like this: "Haslem and Rein represent a real-world American couple who wanted to plan their family the way they thought it best. And the *New York Times*...should be commended for openly discussing abortion in the pages of Vows."

The *Salon* news site called it significant: "It's just eight sentences in the much longer piece, but it's significant to see such a frank discussion of abortion in a wedding announcement."

"Steps forward!" proclaims the sex-saturated women's magazine *Cosmo*. "Couples like Haslem and Rein, whose prenuptial courtship lasted longer than many full-fledged marriages do these days, took steps forward at precisely the time they were ready and made sure that benchmarks in their relationship occurred on their own terms—and that's great to see in the pages of the *Times*."

Enough!

Here's the deal: the secular forces are very aggressive in equipping their own and trying to reach as many as they can with their viewpoint. Are we prepared to winsomely and accurately address this issue in the marketplace? In our neighborhoods, schools, workplaces, and wherever, we must know the proper responses to the arguments that continue to be raised.

In this area under our social justice banner, let's look not only at sonograms revealing the clear and unmistakable preborn, precious baby in the womb, but how we can speak up on their behalf as catalysts for change. We'll look at some of the most common objections that are raised and the proper Biblical responses to help persuade people and save little babies' lives. I encourage you to download this material, keep it on file, and quote it for yourself, your family, your church, and your friends who care about *"speaking up for those who cannot speak for themselves,"* as Proverbs 31:8 tells us.

Let's get started.

Responses to the 10 Most Common Pro-Abortion Arguments

1. "Isn't abortion merely terminating a pregnancy?"

There are two points to consider here.

- First, recognize the euphemism. We shouldn't just say that abortion "terminates a pregnancy." Abortion takes the life of an unborn child. The unborn child is a person, not an abstraction or a "product of conception."

- Second, abortion does not merely "terminate a pregnancy." Can you imagine a headline like this: "Lee Harvey Oswald Terminates Kennedy's Presidency"? At conception, the entire genetic code is present, which determines what a person will look like as an adult. By the eighteenth day, the heart has begun to beat. By the thirtieth day, all major structures of the body are evident and launched for development!

2. "Isn't this a political issue best left to politicians, judges, public-opinion polls or states to decide?"

Actually, this is primarily a moral issue for which we are all accountable. Judeo-Christian foundations in America have always upheld the sanctity of life, and it is only since a Supreme Court decision in 1973 that abortion was considered legal throughout the land. Millions believe this was a tragic error, like prior decisions regarding black Americans, and want to see protection for the unborn restored.

We gasp when someone cites that Adolf Hitler exterminated six million innocent Jews. But unless we see a reversal of this horrendous abortion decision, we will add another five million aborted babies to the statistics on abortion in a few more years, taking us to the sixty million mark. That is 10 times more innocent lives than Hitler took!

3. "Isn't it unfair for a candidate's position on abortion to be a single-issue litmus test to qualify or disqualify him or her for elected office?"

A single issue should not qualify someone for office, but a single issue can disqualify him. This must be examined, since you can judge the character of a person by how he treats those who can do nothing for him. The dignity of human life is, in a sense, a thread that touches upon our life connection with the poor, the elderly, the disabled, the prisoner, the AIDS patient, the sex slave, or any of life's most vulnerable. As advocates for social justice, we stand up and speak up and do whatever is needed through caring appeals, crisis pregnancy centers, adoption, education, and political activism.

To the charge that we are "single-issue voters," simply point out that there are numerous single issues that disqualify a person for office. Endorsements of rape, bribery, corporate fraud, or bigotry are just a few examples. If we have laws forbidding cruelty to animals (ask football star Michael Vick if he realizes the crime to maim, mutilate, or kill an animal is legit), why not the same concern for innocent, unborn little babies?

We don't vote for candidates simply because they uphold the sanctity of life; they must be called and competent. Yet this does reveal a person's moral character and ethics in a very clear way. I personally have a conviction to never support a candidate who endorses abortion. Don't be misled by clever politicians using "War on Women" and "Women's Reproductive Rights" as a smokescreen.

In the midst of a generation celebrating abortions in wedding announcements and where pro-abortionists, including many deceived and cowardly politicians and even pastors, will not speak up for those that are perish-

ing, God is raising up those with courage and conviction
to care for the "least of these" little ones.

4. "What about politicians who say they are pro-life but
don't want to impose their personal views on others?"

This clever attempt to dodge the issue is similar to
someone saying they oppose sexual molestation of children and stalking by predators but don't want to impose
their personal views on others.

5. "Isn't abortion a safe, harmless procedure like other surgeries—say, a root canal or tonsillectomy?"

Absolutely not! It is an operation terminating the
life of a developing little baby. If it was simply like
these two procedures mentioned, why are there so many
post-abortion support groups and scores of women getting professional counseling and grief therapy? Why do
you think the majority of people choose not to even look
at pictures of an abortion or the remains of a dismem-
bered little baby? Have you spoken with or read testimonies of women with abortion-related physical and
psychological problems that cause ongoing remorse and
regret? This is a serious issue. And if you ever watch an
actual video of a late-term abortion where scissors are
inserted into the base of the baby's skull and a behead-
ing occurs in all its gory, barbaric, bloody way (I dare
you!), you'll never be silent again!

6. "Is it love to bring unwanted children into the world where
they will be neglected, abused, and poverty-stricken?"

Just because a pregnancy is initially unwanted or un-
planned does not necessarily mean that the baby will be
unwanted when born. And should the biological parents
not desire to care for their newborn, there are hundreds
of thousands of couples, many who have waited for up
to seven years due to a shortage of available babies, who
are eager to adopt.

Concerning poverty, are we to conclude that death is
better than being poor? Jesus said, "The poor you will
always have with you." But love never takes innocent

human life; rather, love always seeks to heal, to help, and to extend constructive alternatives.

Before her death, Mother Teresa spoke at the National Prayer Breakfast in Washington, DC, with then-President Bill Clinton and his wife, Hillary (a staunch supporter of unfettered abortion), listening at her side. They were and are both "pro-choice." Responding to those who say abortion spares "unwanted" children, the diminutive nun extended her arms and said, "There is no such thing as an unwanted child! Bring any such child to me. I will find them a home!" She later stated, "We cannot fight credibly against other social and moral ills, including poverty and violence, while we tolerate mass killings by abortion." Why don't you reread that last sentence slowly?

7. "Doesn't a woman have the right to control her own body? Isn't this really a war on women?"

In reality, a baby is not just "part of the woman's body" like her liver or lungs. The unborn child is a totally separate person with 46 chromosomes, a separate blood system (often with a totally different blood type), and its own unique body parts.

Beyond this, it must be understood that no person has absolute rights over their own body. All of us are subject to certain civil laws that restrict our personal rights. For example, a woman may not legally sell her body for prostitution; she may not legally inject narcotic drugs into her body; and she may not legally kill herself. In these ways she does not have a total "right" to control her own body. No one does!

Not long ago, the *New York Times Magazine* ran an article about Amy Richards after she learned she was pregnant with triplets. Realizing it would mean "shopping only at Costco and buying big jars of mayonnaise," she asked her obstetrician, "Is it possible to get rid of one of them? Or two of them?"

The article related that Richards's boyfriend balked as he stared at the three pre-born babies on the sonogram. "Oh my gosh," he said. "There are three heart-beats! I can't believe we are about to make two disappear."

Richards fluffed off his request to at least consider having the triplets and aborted the two unborn babies. Without the abortions, she exclaimed, "I'd have to give up my life!"

Richards is the brainchild behind Planned Parent-hood's tee-shirt campaign encouraging ladies to proudly proclaim, "I had an abortion!"

In our culture today, we are seeing misguided freedom run amok. It's time to rein things back in, get back on the truth track, and defend the weak and needy ones—the least of Christ's brethren (Matt. 25:45).

8. "Aren't you trying to impose your morality on others, especially since the Supreme Court made abortion legal?"

There is an incorrect assumption here that nobody should attempt to impose their moral views upon anybody else. This assumption ignores the obvious fact that laws impose morality upon others; for example, it's illegal to steal, to cheat on your income taxes, or to run without clothes through a shopping mall.

The truth is that someone's morality determines the fate of the innocent unborn. God and our Founding Fathers stated that everyone has a "right to life."

Regarding the Supreme Court making abortion legal, that is true. They also declared black people were not citizens but merely property in the Dred Scott decision of 1857. They also upheld the sterilization of certain undesirable people years ago! They were wrong then, and they were wrong again in their abortion decision of 1973. Just as courageous people took a stand then against immoral laws and won victories for justice, so too in our day are we called to take a stand for the defenseless baby in the womb.

9. "With modern technological advances, isn't it best that we prevent a child from being born into the world who may be deformed or handicapped?"

Since when has it become a capital offense to be less than perfect? The assumption here is one that declares, "Children born with deformities or handicaps will not live a fully meaningful life. Theirs will be a miserable existence." No evidence supports this misguided viewpoint.

Consider the names of some who suffered severe handicaps: Helen Keller, blind and deaf; Stevie Wonder, blind from birth; Franklin Delano Roosevelt, crippled from polio; Beethoven, deaf; Stephen Hawking, Lou Gehrig's disease; Christopher Reeve, paralyzed; and Michael J. Fox, Parkinson's disease. Did they live non-meaningful lives?

10. "Do you want abortion forced to back alleys, where tens of thousands of women will once again die?"

Former abortion rights activist Dr. Bernard Nathanson admitted that he and his cofounders of the National Abortion Rights Action League fabricated the figure that one million women were getting illegal abortions in America yearly, with tens of thousands dying. The doctor, who became pro-life before his death and strongly opposed abortion, stated that the average was really about 98,000 illegal abortions, with an average of about 250 deaths for 25 years before 1973. Plus, 90 percent of these were done in doctors' offices, not back alleys! And, yes, some died, as they still do even in our day.

Should we legalize and sanction heroin addiction because some people die in back alleys due to overdoses and dirty needles? Should we legalize and promote prostitution as a legitimate business in order to curb the spread of rape and venereal disease? And remember, the central issue is this: there is another human being whose life is at stake! Don't be deceived by people, especially clever politicians saying they don't like abortion but

let's find common ground to keep it "safe, legal, and
rare." Safe for whom? Not the beautiful baby ready to
come forth!

Here's the deal: In the Colorado flooding of not long ago, it was
mandatory that animals were to be rescued. How can we do any
less for the defenseless unborn? While we pray for and support pro-
life leaders who will speak with clarity on the hot-button issues of
our day, namely abortion and homosexuality, let's engage people
in the marketplace in a charitable yet clear way, answering their
objections with the truth. Remember, Scripture declares that *"...the*
Lord hates...hands that shed innocent blood" (Prov. 6:16-17, KJV).

Can we count you among us?

The Rev. Martin Luther King Jr., who wholeheartedly supported
the sanctity of life, said it best:

> *"Our lives begin to end the day we become silent about*
> *things that matter."*

May we, as courageous Christians, shake off any apathy and
speak out for justice for the unborn. Let's be at the vanguard of a
momentous turnaround that history will record.

Chapter 25
Illegal Immigration

Three Steps to Solve Immigration Problems the Jesus Way
My father was an immigrant who came here from Poland as a child.
We lived a poor life with no car and no vacations; my dad worked
as a janitor and my disabled mother scrubbed floors on her knees
three days a week. I start here because I have real compassion for
immigrants and support immigration—*legal* immigration.

For those harboring images of Jesus as a meek and mild religious
figure with naked baby cherubs encircling His frisbee-haloed head, the
following biblical event may be challenging to consider. It happened as
parents brought their kids to Jesus so He could "touch and bless them"
(Mk 10:13), but His disciples resented the intrusion.

"When Jesus saw this, He became furious and told them, 'Let the
little children come to me...'" (Matt.10:14 ISV). Other translations
say He was "moved with indignation" or "became indignant."

Why the intense display of emotion?

The old classic hymn makes it plain. "Jesus loves the little
children...all the children of the world. Be they yellow, black, or
white, they are precious in His sight. Jesus loves the little children
of the world."

After touching them as a token of affirmation and blessing (today
He'd most likely give them a fist-bump and a high-five!), Jesus did

what He always did after ministering to children—released them back to Dad and Mom.

Though the case could be made that these little ones would certainly fare better leaving parental ties to enjoy a better way of life by following the One who could heal any sickness, feed multitudes, and provide extraordinary instruction, Jesus Christ modeled a maxim throughout His ministry: Express compassion. Honor authority.

A similar standard of conduct relevant to us today would be, "Demonstrate love. Uphold law."

In light of the continuing illegal-immigration and humanitarian crises (exacerbated by the not-long-ago unprecedented surge of over 60,000 children from Central America crossing our border without parental oversight), we'd do well to follow the method of the Master before this steady flood becomes an overwhelming tsunami.

Many well-intentioned but, I believe, misdirected individuals (I respectfully include here presidents and presidential candidates, influential politicians, and news commentators) seem to believe that the compassionate solution to the escalating border crisis is to extend our arms and declare, "Y'all come in!" Guilt is projected on those who sincerely disagree and dare to say, "You're missing it and not handling this the way Jesus would."

Who's right?

W. W. J. D.?

Over four decades ago, I worked at the AFL-CIO headquarters, across the street from the White House. My job was in the Community Relations Department, helping union members and their families with humanitarian needs outside of the union contract. Early on I discovered there were requirements and limitations to assistance being offered.

When I transitioned to vocational ministry, where I've served people's needs for over forty-three years, I read an influential book from 1896, *In His Steps: What Would Jesus Do?* by Charles Sheldon. It's the story of a pastor challenging his church members to spend one full year asking the question "What would Jesus do?" before making any decision.

This classic reinforced what I learned in my union position and in my study of the Gospels: Jesus did not try to meet every need in every place at every time. Need does not necessarily constitute ministry! Like Him, we need to be discerning and determine available resources in dealing with people's legitimate needs.

"Multitudes came together to hear and be healed by Jesus of their infirmities but he withdrew to a lonely place and prayed" (Lk 5:15–16).

If we operate out of sentimentality, Jesus appears to be uncaring and inconsiderate, doesn't he?

In Matthew 22:11-14, Jesus told a parable of a man desiring entrance to an event but refused entrance because of not honoring the requirements.

In Matthew 25:1-13, He told of ten young maidens desiring to gain entrance to a special occasion and yet five were turned away and called "foolish" because they did not fulfill the requirements.

That same chapter cites individuals being given different "talents" but one who failed to do what he was told was called "lazy," had the gift taken away, and was barred from the estate.

In 2 Corinthians 8:12 we have the record of the early Christian community being reminded that giving to the needy in Jerusalem was "according to what a person has, not according to what he does not have." In other words, there are times we need to be realistic regarding our resources.

Boundaries and Borders
When it comes to immigration policy, there are many influential leaders whose philosophy is to have "open borders," removing limitations and giving access to all desiring to come in.

Some cite our motto *"E pluribus unum"* (Out of many, one) and try to strike a sympathetic chord in saying "Don't make it harder for the best and the brightest to come here!"

Those who differ with this approach say that they want America open to those who want to come but let's do it the proper way. And let's be honest and admit that we are mainly bringing the poor, illiterate, sick, and uneducated as well as criminals and potential terrorists, thereby underscoring why it has to be done in a responsible and orderly way. Eighty to ninety percent come to us from Third World countries and the facts show their higher rates of crime, incarceration, spousal abuse, disease, child abuse, drug abuse, dropouts, illiteracy, and obesity. Children are more involved in gangs and they consume record levels of taxpayer-funded social service benefits. What about ISIS infiltration and our security?

"But it's cheap labor, isn't it?!" Yes, but as we'll see, they must do it the right way and not be given illegal entry and entitlements to "pad" the base of a political party, whose strategy is to bring in thirty million new voters! This is *serious*.

While I pray for certain politicians every single day (for forty years I've served as a board member with Intercessors for America, promoting prayer and fasting for our nation), I strongly yet respectfully disagree with the way that many of them have handled the entire crisis over the years.

Former Governor Rick Perry of Texas stated that he explicitly warned Barack Obama in a letter regarding our southern border's chaotic situation. He pled for 1,000 National Guardsmen to secure the border (to no avail) and $500 million to cover the tax money Texans spent because of Obama's inaction. The president's failure to act, plus his rhetoric toward Mexico, El Salvador, Honduras, and Guatemala, suggest that America is wide open to immigrants, especially children, freely coming and not having to worry about deportation. California Democratic Sen. Dianne Feinstein said, "… my staff learned that many of the children were smuggled across the border after hearing radio ads promising they would not be deported."

The word is out on the street that you can come to America, derive all the benefits, and not be sent back. The Breitbart Report revealed that in 2013, ninty-eight percent of minors who came were allowed to stay (DHS-ICE figures).

People across the United States of America from both parties are asking if this was a man-made crisis to garner votes and change Texas into a Democratic state. Remember the philosophy of Obama's former chief of staff, Rahm Emanuel:

> *"You never want a serious crisis to go to waste… It's an opportunity to do things that you think you could not do before."*

Recall Obama's initial pledge to *"fundamentally transform the United States of America"*?

Barack Obama was flanked on both sides by influential people echoing his thinking. Senator Nancy Pelosi of California embraced the idea of open borders without restraints. Democratic columnist and commentator, Kirsten Powers, states emphatically that she supports open borders and believes that we must stop putting limitations and boundaries on people wanting to come here.

Here's the deal: Amidst all the turmoil and confusion, it's time to embrace scriptural counsel from the Good Shepherd who referred to himself as the "Gate," stating, *"I tell you the truth, anyone who sneaks over the wall of the sheepfold rather than going through the gate, must surely be a thief and a robber" (Jn 10:1).*

Three Steps to Solve the Crisis
As we proceed, let's remember that immigration is a very volatile social issue. Character is revealed when we listen respectfully to others with whom we disagree. We must choose to remain civil in the midst of spirited discussion. If we resort to name-calling and arrogant attitudes, we'll experience the inevitable. *"If you bite and devour one another, take heed lest you are consumed by one another" (Gal. 5:15).*

1. Extend genuine love to all immigrants.
    God commands us to love our neighbor as a directive, not an elective. Love is not based on emotion or sentiment but an unselfish choice for the greatest good of another person. As the bumper sticker says, "Love is a verb."
    God directs us to "help the weak and be patient with everyone" (1 Thess. 4:13) and care for the poor, widowed, and orphaned (Jas 1:27-8; Gal. 2:14).
    In the Old Testament, immigrants were to be granted acceptance (Lev. 19:33-4; Ex. 22:21); were given opportunities to collect food (Lev. 19: 9-10); and were to be treated justly (Lev. 1:16). This was not some blanket entitlement, as God required the immigrant to keep the

laws of the land just like the native people (Ex. 12:48-9; Ex. 23:12).

2. Respect realistic limits.

Just as boundaries need to be determined and adhered to on the personal level, so too does this apply on the national level. Disregarding this principle brings disastrous results.

Idealism says, "Open the gates and let everybody in!" Realism says, "Assess our resources and capabilities to responsibly determine what we can do at this particular time."

"Lord, you have assigned me my portion and my cup, you have made my life secure. The boundary lines have fallen for me in pleasant places, surely I have a delightful inheritance" (Ps. 16:5-6).

Individuals who discipline themselves to honor their God-given assignment and boundaries find security, a pleasant life, and a delightful inheritance. This is why the apostle Paul wisely told a church, "We however will not boast beyond proper limits but will confine our boasting to the spheres of service God himself has assigned us, a sphere that also includes you" (2 Cor. 10:13-14).

If a lifeboat has a sign stating "Limit of 12," it may appear compassionate to try and rescue 25 but the result can be the drowning of everyone!

Years ago, one of Christianity's most gifted musicians, Keith Green, tragically decided to risk overloading a plane with additional passengers, including two members of his family. The plane began its ascent but quickly began a descent that brought a devastating crash, killing all on board.

Headlines recently stated that it now takes approximately $130,000 yearly for a family of four to fulfill the American Dream. Assessing their current station in life, a couple decides that two, three, or maybe four children are probably the limit for them. Is it right for someone to chide this couple for not being like the Duggar family with nineteen children? Today America faces $19 trillion in debt. Cities are going bankrupt or are on the precipice of insolvency. The welfare system is exploding. We are stretched to the max in our emergency rooms, schools, health care, and social service agencies.

The *New York Times* said that we added 300,000 more illegal immigrants in one three-month period in 2014! At present, the floodtide shows no signs of receding.

Isn't it common sense that we appeal to those who may be well-intentioned but could be taking us on the path to destruction if we are not responsible in setting realistic limits for immigration before it's too late?

3. Obey the government and its laws.

This point is so plainly simple yet blatantly disregarded; it's embarrassing that it has to be stated!

God tells us, *"If you are willing (consent in your wills) and obedient (carry out the action) you shall eat the good of the land (reap abundant blessings)" (Is 1:19).* One result of obedience is that immigrants shall not devour a nation's crops (see v. 7). Sadly, hasn't this been happening?

It is unmistakable that the divine directive is for citizens to obey the governing authorities (Rom. 13:1-7; 1 Pet. 2:13-14). The one exception is if government forces us to violate a law of God (Acts 5:29). Why is this so difficult for many American citizens and illegal immigrants to grasp? When people argue, "We need to help bring people out of the shadows," there is a reason they're in the shadows in the first place! Scores broke the law and are hiding. Jesus said, *"Everyone who does evil, hates the light, and will not come into the light for fear that his deeds will be exposed." (Jn 3:20)*

In our nation, when citizens sincerely believe that a law is unfair and should be changed, we have the recourse of doing it! Until such time, existing laws need to be obeyed or the result is lawlessness, which we are seeing increasingly in our country.

For the millions of illegal immigrants presently in the United States of America, a bipartisan team of public servants needs to humbly come together to hammer out a pathway to citizenship that does not compromise existing laws or make a mockery of their predecessors who achieved their citizenship the proper way.

Be honest: what is your reaction when you have stood in line for twenty to thirty minutes for a ticket or restaurant seat and someone selfishly barges in line? "Hey! Hey! Excuse me; you need to wait in line like the rest of us!"

This is not an insurmountable task. Local post offices can be used for registration. Illegal immigrants can be told that they have thirty days to comply, receive help in the eight-step process for citizenship, and secure their identification card (green card) attesting to their permanent residence. Sponsors can be invited to come forth and serve as a "big brother" or "big sister," supporting our immigrant friends who are understandably insecure and apprehensive. And yes, failure to comply would result in fines and/or possible jail time to impress upon individuals the seriousness of getting this done once and for all. Only then can we as the American family begin to put this unfortunate chapter behind us to find a brighter future.

"But, Larry, this would probably cost money. Can we afford it?"

Barack Obama, not long ago, asked for $3.7 billion to basically alleviate the humanitarian crisis on our southern border (which should never have happened in the first place!). Only 1.8% of this sum was suggested for bolstering border security, which is critical to resolving this crisis and avoiding similar crises like this in the future.

Why don't we direct a larger amount to support the immediate training of qualified Border Patrol agents; deploy at least 1,000 National Guard troops to the southern border; and utilize daily drone flights along the border to identify those involved in human trafficking and drug cartels?

We must—I say it again—we must build up and extend the long-overdue border fence. Yes, walls and fences do work; if they don't, why do we have them around the White House? Israel and China have relied on them for centuries.

The Great Wall of China is 13,000 miles long and was built centuries before Christ, and it works for them! When elitists who live in gated communities tell us "Fences don't work!" I ask, then why do they have them?! As Ann Coulter, author of ten *New York Times* bestsellers puts it, "When the bathtub is overflowing, the very first thing you do is: *Turn off the water*. You don't debate whether to use a rag or a mop...The number one priority is: Shut off the water!

Finally, allocate generous amounts to compensate the kindhearted citizens who respond to the call for a national sponsorship service corps.

Come on. Let's get going and get this done! Projections for unaccompanied immigrant children are currently 90,000 for one year and 150,000 for the next year! The heinous crime of human trafficking is epidemic. Parentless children warehoused in close-knit conditions are an invitation for abuse of every kind, plus a breeding ground for communicable diseases like polio, tuberculosis, influenza, and measles. This public health risk is only exceeded by the national security risk of terrorists and drug cartel members slipping into our nation to link with sleeper cells. ISIS is real!

Reckless and lax enforcement of immigration and deportation laws must be stopped. In 2013, ICE (Immigration Customs Enforcement) allegedly released 36,007 convicted criminals awaiting deportation. Over one hundred had homicide convictions and others had convictions for kidnapping and sexual assaults. Things are at a critical "threat level" and social justice—caring for our own families and society at large—demands action now! (For further info read *Adios, America! The Left's Plan to Turn Our Country Into a Third World Hellhole* by author and syndicated columnist Ann Coulter [Regnery Publishing, 2015]).

This is a pivotal time and a defining moment in our history. We need a unified response here in America and among our Central American partners who need to know that we will severely curtail financial aid if they fail to cooperate. One leader has even called for a boycott of Mexico tourism until they comply.

Jesus loves all the little children of the world. He modeled the maxim of demonstrating love and honoring authority.

We've squandered enough time and treasure trying things our way. It's time we humble ourselves and embrace the method of the Master in this area of social justice.

Chapter 26
Capital Punishment

Botched Execution: A Reason to Ban Capital Punishment?
Social justice entails the proper treatment of prisoners. Jesus told us in Matthew 25:36 that "I was in prison and you came to visit me." Visiting someone who's a prisoner is one thing but what about the controversial area of capital punishment? We need a Biblical worldview.

Scripture, not sentiment, must direct the life of an authentic Christian. Misdirected mercy can seem right but it oftentimes entails disobedience to God's clear directives. This is especially relevant regarding the death penalty.

Not long ago, a story about a mishandled execution blazed across the Internet and newspapers in America. Once again we hear individuals lifting their voices that it is time to do away with the death penalty once and for all! These stories occur with increasingly regularity.

In case you missed what happened, here's a facsimile version conveyed by "bleeding hearts." The purpose: to evoke sympathy, stir emotions, and raise opposition to the "barbaric and archaic" death penalty still allowed in America.

"A young black man, a victim of an unfortunate environment, was involved in a crime a while ago where a teenager lost her life.

He did not personally kill the girl but admittedly was complicit in telling his friends to do something that resulted in her death."

A subsequent tragedy occurred when the confused man suffered immensely because the mixture of administered drugs administered in his execution did not take effect quickly. This caused him great pain as he contorted on a gurney, struggling to speak, after he had been declared unconscious. One can only imagine the excruciating pain and torture that this unfortunate individual experienced until he eventually suffered a massive heart attack and died.

"This unnecessary brutality in our criminal justice system must stop. May what happened in Oklahoma be a rallying cry so the 32 states still murdering people through the death penalty act swiftly and change their laws. Intelligent and compassionate people must arise and cause others to come to their senses in abolishing the death penalty in the United States of America."

Now what's the real story? And is capital punishment a just, legitimate, and Biblical way to administer justice? If we uphold the "sanctity of life" shouldn't we speak up for victims like this poor man and stop promoting violence?

Here's the deal: Clayton Lockett was loved by God as a sinner like every one of us. Jesus Christ died on a cross for him and took the judgment he deserved. He rose from the dead so all mankind can be redeemed through His shed blood if we repent and put our faith in Him as our Lord and Savior. At this point, we do not know if he placed his full trust in Jesus to save him. Most likely a chaplain counseled him prior to his scheduled execution and we hope that he humbled himself to receive God's mercy prior to his death.

Something we do know is that Lockett and his accomplices abducted two teenagers plus a man and his baby. He shot the young girl with a shotgun and when she did not die he directed his partners to bury her alive.

Here's the summary of his crimes:

- First-degree murder

- First-degree burglary

- Three counts of assault with a dangerous weapon

- Three counts of forcible oral sodomy

- Four counts of first-degree rape

- Four counts of kidnapping

- Four counts of robbery by force

Clayton acknowledged making the young woman watch as her grave was dug and killing her in this heinous way. There was no question of his guilt or of his sanity.

The full story to this botched execution helps bring things into perspective. What if nineteen-year-old Stephanie Nieman were your daughter? Would you shrug off the crime and desire leniency or do you think you would cry out for justice with every fiber of your being, while knowing your Christian duty to forgive?

Sweeping aside any gut-wrenching, emotional reaction to a crime such as the above, let's deal with the question from a Biblical worldview. "Does God mandate the execution of a convicted murderer?"

While individual Christians are called to forgive those who repent and refrain from vengeance, governing authorities are entrusted with the responsibility of taking the life of an individual who has been convicted of willful murder. Whether it is individuals perpetrating the Boston Marathon bombing, terrorists on 9/11, serial killers, aircraft hijackers, deranged people using weapons of mass destruction, or espionage that jeopardizes countless citizens, God directs the taking of life when a criminal is found guilty. The same holds for the average man or woman found guilty of premeditated murder.

In Genesis 9:5b-6, God's directive in this matter does not cheapen but rather elevates the dignity of human life. Why? Killing another human being is a direct attack against God Himself for every person is created "in the image of God."

> *"And from each man, too, I will demand an accounting for the life of his fellow man. Whoever sheds the blood of a man, by man shall his blood be shed; for in the image of God has God made man."*

The divine decree is that if an individual takes the life of another human being, he or she must pay the ultimate price—forfeiting one's life as punishment.

Whom does God entrust to carry out this act of justice? In the New Testament, in Romans 13:1-5, we discover that it is the civil authorities:

> *Everyone must submit himself to the governing authorities, for there is no authority except that which God has established. The authorities that exist have been established by God. Consequently, he who rebels against the authority is rebelling against what God has instituted, and those who do so will bring judgment on themselves. For rulers hold no terror for those who do right, but for those who do wrong. Do you want to be free from fear of the one in authority? Then do what is right and he will commend you. For he is God's servant to do you good. But if you do wrong, be afraid for he does not bear the sword for nothing. He is God's servant, an agent of wrath to bring punishment on the wrongdoer. Therefore, it is necessary to submit to the authorities, not only because of possible punishment but also because of conscience.*

These two sections of scripture are foundational for understanding the Biblical worldview on the death penalty. The Greek word for "sword" is used repeatedly in the New Testament to speak of the instrument by which people are put to death.

1 Peter 2:13-14 reinforces this Biblical principle: *"Submit yourselves for the Lord's sake to every authority instituted among men: whether to the king, as the supreme authority, or to governors, who are sent by Him to punish those who do wrong and to commend those who do right."*

The primary functions of righteous and legitimate civil government are simple:

1. Promote good.

2. Punish evil.

And for those who might object, saying that this is taking revenge on people rather than demonstrating Christian love, we need to remind ourselves that discipline is an expression of God's love (Heb. 12:6). Let's also remind ourselves of what Scripture tells us clearly in Romans 12:19: *"Do not take revenge, my friends, but leave room for God's wrath, for it is written: 'It is mine to avenge, I will repay…'"*

Clearly stated, we should never seek to take personal revenge on others when we have been seriously wronged, but we should pray and seek justice being administered through the workings of civil authorities.

In the last book of the Bible we have the account of individuals who were free from any trace of sin and yet they looked to God to avenge those who had murdered them: *"When he opened the fifth seal, I saw under the altar the souls of those who had been slain because of the Word of God and the testimony they had maintained. They called out in a loud voice, 'How long, Sovereign Lord, holy and true, until You judge the inhabitants of the earth and avenge our blood?'" (Rev. 6:9-10)*

Even Paul the apostle understood the reality of capital punishment, if he deserved it, when he stood appealing to Caesar for justice. *"If, however, I am guilty of doing anything deserving death, I do not refuse to die. But if the charges brought against me by these Jews are not true, no one has the right to hand me over to them. I appeal to Caesar!" (Acts 25:11).*

Some people falsely believe that the death penalty is not a deterrent to murder. They produce scant evidence to support their argument.

The reality is this: most criminals know their chance of being put to death is minimal so they rationalize that they can get away with their crimes. Appeals drag on for decades instead of governing authorities dealing swiftly and decisively with capital crimes. Also, many lawbreakers observe lenient judges who give the proverbial "slap on the wrist" so they think they'll get a break if caught. "Young lady, for the serious crime of suffocating your two-year-old twins, I sympathize with your condition of being tired and strung out on meth. Therefore, I sentence you to three years on probation, therapy, six weeks of anger-management classes, rehabilitation counseling, plus a year of community service. Case dismissed." Whaaat?!

What does God warn about slowly administering punishment to the guilty? *"Because the sentence against an evil deed is not*

executed speedily, the heart of the children of man is fully set to do
evil" (Eccl. 8:11).

From the grave we should listen afresh to the founder of the
FBI, J. Edgar Hoover, who once said, *"Experience has clearly*
demonstrated, however, that the time-proven deterrents to crime are
sure detection, swift apprehension, and proper punishment. Each
is a necessary ingredient. Law-abiding citizens have a right to
expect that the efforts of law enforcement officers in detecting and
apprehending criminals will be followed by realistic punishment."

While Jesus wanted the men He discipled to carry a weapon for
self-defense (Luke 22:36-38; Matt. 26:52) and deter a criminal. He
taught them certain things are to be "rendered unto Caesar" such as
we've laid out in this commentary.

Were there botched executions in the time of Jesus Christ?
Who knows? We do know He would have been faithful to divine
revelation as long as we live in this fallen world.

Maranatha. Come quickly Lord Jesus!

Chapter 27
Corporal Punishment (Spanking)

Should Children be Spanked?

"Jesus loves the little children...all the children of the world. Be they yellow, black or white, they are precious in His sight. Jesus loves the little children of the world."

Recall this familiar childhood hymn? Seeing little ones together singing it while adjusting their underwear, picking their noses, or simply standing statue-like, having forgotten the words, conjures up images of their innocence and our need to simply encourage them in their perfection. Until...

- Little Joey socks sweetie Suzy in the nose.

- Princess Priscilla screams "I won't!" ten times in a row when asked to retrieve her toys.

- Mischievous Mickey defies your order and continues pouring your expensive perfume down the drain.

In these young, formative years when children are like wet cement, what's a parent to do? Someone said, "It's better to build children than repair men," but how? Does God give us the tools? Does social justice include looking out for children's welfare, including the thorny topic of discipline? Even if you are single or without children now, listen up and learn these essentials.

In the last laps of our Bullseye Challenge we need to examine this area which is becoming increasingly delicate in our culture.

Corporal punishment is a sensitive subject. Charges brought not long ago against a popular NFL running back brought it to the surface once again.

Decades ago I authored a book now titled *The Little Handbook of Loving Correction*. It was formerly called *God, the Rod, and Your Child's Bod*. I changed it out of cultural sensitivity.

This subject is very personal to me because I actually had a family member bring totally false accusations against me regarding this issue! A church I cofounded over thirty-eight years ago was embroiled in a lawsuit dealing with "abuse" and even though I departed the church twenty-four years ago, my name was "thrown in the hopper."

Have you ever disciplined a child by confining them to their room until they changed their attitude ("imprisonment")? Did you ever instruct a child that there would be no lunch until they completed all their chores ("food deprivation")? How about spankings to correct ongoing, defiant behavior ("beatings and abuse")?

Thankfully the judge dismissed the case. They were blatantly false accusations. But episodes like this and current news reporting causes confusion among parents who are trying to be faithful in raising their children according to Biblical standards.

Here's the deal: Scripture tells us that *"the corrections of discipline are the way to life" (Prov. 6:23).* What we need is a clear Biblical worldview on the subject of corporal punishment so both parent and child enjoy that result.

Realism vs. Idealism in Raising Kids

Raising children requires a realistic perspective on our inherited sinful nature and a rejection of the "inherent goodness of man." Adam rebelled and all of us have ratified that rebellion because of our inherited sinful nature.

We don't have to teach children to be selfish, lie, hit their siblings, steal, or pout when they don't get their way. We do have to train them to learn to control themselves and do what is right in the sight of God and man.

Don't you just love it when so-called marriage and parenting "experts" expound their views on TV in their world of Utopia? One gorgeous celebrity has been divorced four times and yet goes on the circuit to promote her new book on romance and happy marriage (no jiving!). Another couple who are living together with no children confidently share their "wisdom" philosophy about raising their future children by simply reasoning with them, calmly affirming them, and consistently building up their self-esteem.

Yeah, right. Wait until they confront strong-willed little Grayson in all his glorious disobedience and defiance one day! This is why seasoned veterans chuckle at this idealism and understand bumper stickers reading: "Insanity is inherited. You get it from your children."

If you permit a child to nurture destructive habits, which they will one day be forced (with greater difficulty) to break, you are living beneath the revealed will of God concerning your role as a parent.

There is a difference between abusing a child and disciplining a child. Children know the difference between an objective spanking administered in love and a beating springing from hostility and anger.

- *"Correct your son, and he shall give you rest; yes, he shall give delight unto your soul"* (Pr. 29:17).

- "Foolishness is bound in the heart of the child; but the rod of correction shall drive it from him" (Pr. 22:15).

- "By mere words a servant is not disciplined, for though he understands, he will not give heed" (Pr. 29:19).

- "The rod and reproof give wisdom, but a child left to himself brings shame to his mother" (Pr. 29:15).

- "Do not withhold discipline from a child; if you punish him with the rod, he will not die. Punish him with the rod and save his soul from death" (Pr. 23:13).

- "Train a child in the way he should go, and when he is old he will not turn from it" *(Pr. 22:6)*.

God's method for curbing harmful attitudes and nurturing healthy ones does not involve parents going ballistic, threatening, screaming, or hauling off and smacking in anger. Nor does it involve tuning out destructive conduct, bribing with candy, or banishment to a room to brood and fester in resentment.

Loving correction, which includes spanking at times, is an expression of love! Have you ever experienced a metaphorical "spanking" from the Lord for persistent, ungodly conduct? *"My son, do not make light of the Lord's discipline, and do not lose heart when He rebukes you, because the Lord disciplines those He loves, and He punishes everyone He accepts as a son" (Heb. 12:5-6).*

The 10 Essentials of Loving Correction
Research reveals that, in Americ, a up to eighty-five percent of people acknowledge that they've used corporal punishment. Every state in America allows corporal punishment of children. Nineteen states employ it in the schools. Two hundred thousand students are paddled annually in America according to the US Department of Education. Due to disciplinary problems in schools many are reevaluating their policies like the Arlington school district outside Memphis, Tennessee that just voted recently to reinstate corporal punishment saying, "Teachers need all tools possible."

Prof. Robert Larzelere of Oklahoma State University, who studied this subject for decades, states: "Bac-up spanking done calmly and in a consistent manner with defiant two- to six-year-olds, backing up milder forms of discipline like timeouts, is shown to be effective at changing behavior."

Marjorie Gunnoe at Calvin College in Grand Rapids, Michigan states from her research that "children spanked in a calm, consistent manner have better outcomes than children who have never been spanked."

Former NBA superstar, Charles Barkley, joked recently, "If corporal punishment is a crime, then every black parent in the South is going to be put in jail!"

Recently Dennis Miller, radio host and *Saturday Night Alive* alumnus, suggested on nationwide TV that spanking is a viable solution for out-of-control youth. Referring to two Colorado teenage girls caught trying to defect to ISIS, he stated, "We need to spank again! In my day rebelling was going from the Beatles to the Stones. Now this. I'd put them over my knee and spank 'em!"

Here's some practical guidance to help all of us keep things in perspective regarding loving correction of our children. May the acrostic for CORRECTION serve you well.

C. *Clarity*: Loving correction always begins by clearly defining and communicating reasonable boundaries before they are enforced.

O. *Obedience*: Spankings can occur if Ephesians 6:1(*"Children, obey your parents in the Lord, for this is right"*) is violated.

R. *Right attitudes*: We are to *"serve the Lord with gladness" (Ps. 100:2)*, so persistent whining and complaining has to be addressed.

R. *Restoration*: Embracing and reassuring a child afterwards enables us to avoid leaving them feeling guilty, rejected, or unwanted.

E. *Explanation*: Taking time to explain the offense as well as enabling the parent to calm down (if needed) makes this essential.

C. *Consistency*: Loving correction requires an investment and persevering commitment...*"He who loves him is diligent to discipline him" (Prov. 13:24)*.

T. *Thoroughness*: Shaping the will without breaking the spirit requires being authoritative (not authoritarian) so the child experiences some pain, versus simple "love pats." *"Chasten thy son while there is hope, and let not thy soul spare for his crying" (Prov. 19:18 KJV)*. *"For the moment all discipline seems painful rather than pleasant..." (Heb. 12:11)*.

I. *Immediately*: With some exceptions, loving correction should be given in the moment, not "when Daddy comes home," etc. *"Because sentence against an evil deed is not executed speedily, the heart of the sons of men is fully set to do evil" (Eccl 8:11)*.

O. *Out of Sight*: Discipline is administered in private so as to not humiliate or embarrass a child.

N. Neutral Object: Scripture calls for the use of a "rod (a small, flexible branch) of correction," not a hairbrush, belt, or the nearest object. Hands should be instruments expressing affection and tenderness; we don't want children flinching or retreating when a hand is raised.

A closing question: "Where is the rod administered?"

God in his wisdom prepared a strategic place on the anatomy of our toddlers and children which has ample cushiony, fatty tissue and sensitive nerve endings to respond to Spirit-led stimulation. This "seat of learning" is located at the base of the back, above the thighs, located directly on the bottom of every child. In forty-three years of ministry, I've discovered that all children come equipped with one! *"On the lips of him who has understanding wisdom is found, but a rod is for the back of him who lacks sense" (Prov. 10:13).*

In the final analysis, you as a parent must seek God and His will in the raising of your little "munchkins." If you choose to follow the wisdom of His Word in this area, remember the imaginary "bullseye" is on the fanny, not the face!

Chapter 28
AIDS, Gays, and STDs

Are you ready for what may be the most sensitive yet most urgent topic in our Bullseye Challenge? It comes under social justice, because if we truly care about a fellow human being, we don't avoid potentially inflammatory issues when people's very lives are at stake. And make no mistake about it—people are dying and suffering debilitating diseases because of ignorance and misinformation here. We're not "bigots" or "homophobic" when we lovingly try to warn people about high-risk sexual behavior reaped through LGBT involvement.

When AIDs first was recognized it was called GRID—Gay-Related Immune Deficiency. Other medical authorities labeled it the "Gay Plague." When homosexuals objected to being stigmatized, "names were changed to protect the innocent," or should we say "guilty" in this case?

I cared for and subsequently officiated at the funeral of my friend, John, a former gay man transformed by Christ's love yet destroyed by AIDS. I spoke, as he requested, to his gay and lesbian friends and his daughter at the tearful memorial service. I say this so the reader knows I really do care and when I share the following it is in hopes of rescuing people from disease, devastation, and premature death. Read on.

Why Most Homosexual Love Stories Don't Have Happy Endings
On newsstands across America, *Entertainment Weekly* invited
us to purchase the latest issue, highlighting the "most important,
infuriating, heartbreaking movie of the year." Five sober-faced
celebrities, including Julia Roberts, graced the cover along with
chilling stats intended to shock sensibilities:

- 60%: the percentage of young Americans living with
  HIV today who are unaware that they're infected

- 36 million: the number of people who have died of
  AIDS since 1981

- 22%: the increase in new HIV infections among gay
  and bisexual men in the United States from 2008 to
  2010

- 1994: the year AIDS became the leading cause of
  death among Americans ages 25 to 44.

The cover story inside had the title "This Love Story Does Not Have
a Happy Ending." It told of the central character, who sees his own
body disintegrate and how the movie was the semiautobiographical
story of Larry Kramer, an HIV-positive homosexual who wrote the
play *The Normal Heart.* The article featured a picture of a sickly Mr.
Kramer, who could not contribute to the article because of illness. A
decade ago, he spoke a gloomy message to the LGBTQ community
in New York, some of which follows below. He is the author of the
novel *Faggots* and acknowledges that he previously had tried to kill
himself. Larry Kramer has been a prophetic voice for thirty-seven
years warning of homosexuality's health hazards. He is director of
ACT UP whose slogan is: "Silence = Death."

Here is an excerpt of the message he gave about ten years ago:

> *I have recently gone through my diaries of the worst of
> the AIDS plague years. I saw day after day a notation
> of another friend's death. I listed all the ones I'd slept
> with. There were a couple hundred. Was it my sperm that
> killed them, that did the trick? It is no longer possible
> for me to avoid this question of myself. Have you ever
> wondered how many men you killed? I know I murdered*

some of them. I just know. You know how you sometimes know things? I know. Several hundred over a bunch of years, I have to have murdered some of them, planting in them the original seed. I have put this to several doctors. Mostly they refused to discuss it, even if they are gay. Most doctors do not like to discuss sex or what we do or did. ... They play blind. God knows what they must be thinking when they examine us. Particularly if they aren't gay. One doctor answered me, it takes two to tango so you cannot take the responsibility alone. But in some cases it isn't so easy to answer so flippantly. The sweet young boy who didn't know anything and was in awe of me. I was the first man who [expletive] him. I think I murdered him. The old boyfriend who did not want to go to bed with me and I made him. The man I let [expletive] me because I was trying to make my then boyfriend, now lover, jealous. I know, by the way, that that other one is the one who infected me. You know how you sometime know things? I know he infected me. I tried to murder myself on that one.

Harmful Health Risks of a Homosexual Lifestyle

Recently, the Centers for Disease Control and other reputable agencies have released more findings on homosexual activity. Consider these as we witness the constant barrage of smiling images of the likes of Ellen DeGeneres, Michael Sam, the Cam and Mitchell characters on TV's *Modern Family* (now celebrating their same-sex marriage), or gay actor Neil Patrick Harris standing ninety-eight percent nude on the cover of *Rolling Stone*, promoting his Broadway play about a transvestite in full drag.

Here's the deal: with all the hoopla about this one and that one "coming out" and it being the time to celebrate gay marriage and the gay lifestyle as normal, natural, and beautiful, people need to awaken to the reality that this so-called love story does not have a happy ending. All the safe-sex techniques and medical advancements are not solving the problem either.

- Homosexual and bisexual men account for seventy-five percent of syphilis infections.

- Seventy-eight percent of all new HIV infections are among males, primarily homosexuals.

- Over twenty-five percent of all HIV infections in the United States are among young males ages thirteen to twenty-four.

- The *Journal of Sex Research* reports, "Although heterosexuals outnumber homosexuals by a ratio of at least 20 to 1, homosexual pedophiles commit about one-third of the total number of child sex offenses."

- *Psychological Reports* and the *International Journal of Epidemiology* reported the same findings: Homosexuals have a twenty-year-shorter lifespan.

- It's not a mystery why the FDA banned homosexual male blood donations or why so many homosexuals suffer from what is medically known as gay bowel syndrome and herpes lesions in the mouth.

- The CDC states that over 110 million Americans now have a sexually transmitted disease causing suffering, embarrassment, cancers, relationship problems, and marital discord. Gays are center stage.

Depending on the source, homosexual men have an average lifetime number of sexual partners falling anywhere between 250 to 500. Engaging in sodomy with the "sewage system" of another's anatomy is contrary to God's design and brings inevitable consequences.

Dr. Frank Spinelli wrote the following in the homosexual publication *The Advocate:*

> *Imagine for a moment that you're a doctor—a gay doctor with a practice that predominantly treats gay men. Now guess how many texts and phone calls you might receive during any given weekend involving questions that have to do with recreational drugs, penile discharge, or the risk of contracting HIV from unprotected sexual encounters? Now take that number and multiply it by 10 if that weekend should occur around Gay Pride, Folsom*

Street Fair, Gay Days at Disney, or any one of the Atlantis cruises. Welcome to my world!

God designed a natural order that has men and women coupled together in marriage for the dual purpose of oneness and offspring. Same-sex unions cannot fully deliver on these two, so we are left with the element of pleasure alone. This may or may not last for long, which explains why there are so many multiple partnerships in the homosexual experience (with some rare exceptions) as well as promiscuity and resultant AIDS/HIV/STDs.

Remember your Tinkertoys as a child? They fit together. No matter how hard they try, two gay men or gay women can't. The entire animal kingdom functions the same way in accordance with nature's design. While some folks point to some extremely rare exceptions, where some animals may dabble in homosexual–like activity, keep in mind that they are animals operating out of instinct, not human beings operating out of intellect.

Charity and Clarity Can Make for a Happy Ending
In spite of the gay avalanche upon us, we must lovingly and uncompromisingly hold the line by remaining faithful to Scripture. Practicing homosexuality is sin, and that will never change. To say we genuinely care about our fellow man yet not "speak the truth in love" is cowardice.

A few years ago, my wife noticed a red lesion on my back, and she encouraged me to check it out with a dermatologist. He assessed it as pre-cancerous and subsequently removed it by burning it off my back.

There were four elements that brought me through to a happy ending: honest assessment, pain experienced, affliction eradicated, and health restored.

Would the doctor have been a true healer and friend if he sidestepped the root problem out of fear that he'd offend me and instead merely applied a bandage to my sore, sending me on my way? I could be dead today from his nicety minus the necessity of truth-telling!

The spiritual, emotional, mental, and physical well-being of homosexuals should be every God-fearing person's concern. Being

called a bigot or homophobic must not deter or intimidate us.
Should we shrink back from reaching out in love, the result will
be multitudes succumbing to deception and never discovering how
God designed for us to live "happily ever after" in alignment with
Him.

Chapter 29
Legalizing Marijuana

Seven Reasons to Reject Legalization

The idea of social justice calls for us to look out for the whole of society, especially those most vulnerable. There is underfoot in America a pernicious development to legalize and glamorize smoking "pot" under the ruse of "medical marijuana." "Hey, people suffering and sick need medical relief and weed fits the bill!"

Is this legit? Are impressionable youth exempt from negative consequences? Is the legalization of dope (no pun intended) harmless? Are there other safe, medicinal options?

Because we're called to be "salt" (preserving from decay) and "light" (illuminating the darkness), let's examine seven reasons for rejecting the legalization of marijuana.

"They just found my daughter dead!" This unexpected and startling revelation jolted my morning. At the mall where I exercise, a middle-aged mother darted from the Starbucks and stammered the above words. "Larry, remember when I asked you to pray for my twenty-seven-year-old daughter a couple months ago? A guy came into her life ...This was her first real boyfriend... He made her feel special... He also introduced her to 'getting high.' She'd never done drugs! It wasn't hard stuff–just recreational. Now she's dead! This wasn't supposed to happen!"

I took her hand and we prayed together. Reassuring her as best as I could, I then slipped away, saddened by the tragic news of this mother's only child now gone.

I have a daughter too. For seven years she worked long hours in a youth venue where over a thousand young people came weekly. She regularly shared with us how many were trying pot, leading them down a path to inevitable consequences that broke her heart and brought devastation to them and their families.

Most of us by now have read the news that marijuana was officially declared legal for recreational use in Colorado, as it now is in Washington State. Portland, Maine and Lansing, Michigan and other localities have jumped on the bandwagon too. Initiatives to legalize and legitimize toking up for innocent fun are being pushed nationwide.

A Pendulum is Swinging

In 1969, Americans opposed the legalization of marijuana by an overwhelming one-to one majority. Now more than half of Americans support it; two thirds of those are eighteen to thirty-four!

Is this a good thing?

An ancient proverb gives us a heads up: *"A prudent man sees danger and hides himself. The fool goes on and suffers for it" (Prov. 22:3).* My childhood best friend of over twenty years ignored this advice and was dead before the age of thirty. Like a Cheech and Chong character, he naïvely thought that casual drug use was harmless, following the anthem "All I wanna do is have some fun."

How about you? Consider the following before you are misled by blind leaders of whom Jesus forewarned, *"If the blind lead the blind, both shall fall into the ditch" (Matt. 15:14).*

A line from the classic Eagles song, "Hotel California," serves as ample warning as we proceed: "You can check out any time you like, but you can never leave."

Seven Reasons to Reject the Legalization of Marijuana

1. Don't be duped.
   Our Founding Father, George Washington, told us *"An uninformed populace is easily enslaved."* Address-

ing arguments for legalizing marijuana demands discernment and the ability to recognize a pig with lipstick on.

The "Yes We Cannabis!" movement is out in full force. Advocates and lobbyists are aggressive and persuasive, but misguided and dishonest to the core. Like same-sex marriage proponents, they tell us it's time to be "enlightened...progressive...cool...shake off the old-school mentality and reject everything discriminatory and restrictive in our culture. After all, Amsterdam has joints available alongside coffee in shops throughout their country! We need to get with the program!" (Ask Willie Nelson if he's reconsidering weed after recent stem-cell therapy to save his lungs!)

- "It'll balance the budget... save the economy...create scores of jobs!" In reality, this represents no more than a drop in the bucket, while conveniently ignoring other economic realities.

- "It eliminates the need for law enforcement plus provides needed tax revenue." A whole new set of rules and regulations have to be established and enforced; most people don't voluntarily pay taxes out of sheer civic duty.

- "This won't affect youth... it's only for 21 and up... private use only... since you can grow it at home it won't go out...It's not sold on the streets." Who are we kidding? Look at all the scrambling going on in Colorado as people get around all the so-called rules and authorities turn a blind eye to what's really going on. Clever operators use limos with "free" pot. Drug dealers buy the weed and sell it to support habits. Are signs really effective in airports saying don't take any home? Within twenty-four hours of legalization, a two-year-old girl ended up in the hospital after eating a marijuana cookie.

- "It's for cancer patients." So-called "medical marijuana," for the most part, can be chalked up to trumped-up "stress" and "pain relief" excuses; scores simply want it legalized so they can get stoned, avoid jail, party, and make some fast cash. Los Angeles has already closed 200 "marijuana clinics" because of this travesty while Holland, Portugal, and Zürich, Switzerland, are changing drug policies because of social problems exploding.

- "Marijuana is not addictive... It's like a beer...harmless... It's not as bad as cocaine or heroin." We'll address these but here's the deal as best conveyed by an expert. Dr. Ed Gogek, a Democrat and addiction gsychiatrist, wrote in the *New York Times*: *"I've spent 25 years as a doctor treating drug abusers and they are con artists... Marijuana activists are phony scientists. For years they said marijuana is good for glaucoma when it actually worsens it. They said it is not addictive and this is false! They said it doesn't increase usage among teenagers and all evidence says the opposite...It is not harmless! Youth do worse in school and have two times the dropout rate while marijuana permanently lowers their IQ."*

2. Your health matters.

Our Declaration of Independence refers to God as our Creator. He designed us in His image, directing us to care for our bodies and avoid destructive influences. Why? So we glorify Him in what He calls a *"temple"* which we have *"received from God. You are not your own; you were bought at a price. Therefore honor God with your body" (1Cor. 6:19-20).*

Just as you would not put gunky, contaminated oil into an expensive Lexus, so too are we to steer clear of polluting our body with toxic elements that bring about a premature demise.

If they were able to have a second chance, do you think celebrities like Amy Winehouse, Whitney Houston, Michael Jackson, and multitudes of others who met their tragic end from drugs would encourage you to get started by lighting up a joint? We only pray that in their final moments they repented and got their lives right with a merciful and just God.

In Revelation 22:15, God tells us that "drug users and spellcasters"(CEB) or "sorcerers"(KJV) are under the wrath of God and associated with "dogs"—an idiom for despicable persons. Their severe punishment is separation from God for all eternity. The Greek word used here is *"pharmakeus,"* from which we get our word "pharmaceuticals." Thayer's dictionary defines this as "one who prepares or uses magical remedies."

In Jesus's weakest moment on the cross, He deliberately refused any mind-altering intoxicant that was offered to Him (Matt. 27:34). He serves as our example, not singers, movie stars, and even politicians who persuade multitudes to use drugs.

THC, the active component in marijuana plants (the cause of people getting "high"), is ten times as potent as the "weed "of decades ago (*60 Minutes* special report, 2015). Just like inhaling toxic cigarette smoke, it adversely affects the lungs. In fact, three joints is the equivalent of twenty cigarettes; plus, consider how long people hold it inside. This is why scientific studies have disclosed that three joints a day does as much damage to the lungs as 200 cigarettes!

Smoking cigarettes kills 400,000 Americans every year. Fifty thousand die from secondhand smoke. Eight-point-six million citizens have illnesses caused directly by smoking. Cigarette smoking cuts lives short by an average of thirteen years. Daily misleading and deceptive ads lure multitudes down this path. Guess what unseen entity is trying to do something similar by promoting marijuana?

There are over thirty scientific studies that show a higher risk of schizophrenia and paranoia amongst marijuana users. It increases one's heart rate, producing a five-fold increase in heart attacks and panic attacks.

Some people scoff at statements like these and say they're merely "scare tactics." Do you want to risk your future by relying on "potheads," pop stars, and politicians? These pied pipers will one day be accountable to God for their reckless and irresponsible ways.

3. Avoid deception.

TV and movies abound with stories about demons, the paranormal, vampires, zombies, and the unseen evil realm. It's real and Jesus Christ told us that our spiritual adversary "comes as a thief to steal, kill and destroy" (John 10:10). The Bible clearly warns us not to be "ignorant of his devices" (2 Cor. 2:11).

As America drifts from our Judeo-Christian roots and standards, people's perceptions of marijuana have changed drastically—especially among impressionable youth.

Scores of teenagers have been deceived to view the drug as harmless. Therefore, more are indulging. In 2013, one in fifteen high school seniors reported using marijuana daily. ten years ago, it was one in fifty! This most recent national survey also revealed that only forty percent of high school seniors now believe that smoking marijuana is risky, compared to seventy-five percent twenty years ago.

The delusion is not only in their perception of the drug but in their penchant to partake of it as a means of escape. Why not? "It's legal, or soon will be... It's increasingly available... Pop stars I admire use it, sing, and joke about it and even promote it... Gimme a joint!"

Young people struggling through the teen years, instead of turning to God or their parents or godly counselors, find it easier to escape problems and depression by medicating with drugs like marijuana since it's becoming such an easy solution. The snare is when the "buzz" wears off and a pattern develops of grabbing another joint or experimenting with harder drugs. Soon one is addicted and then it's either more drugs or maybe yield to those persistent suicidal thoughts to simply end it all.

As in the classic film *The Wizard of Oz*, when Dorothy pulled back the curtain and exposed the deceiving mastermind behind the facade, will multitudes take head of the facts being presented and rise up to resist the pull into destruction? More importantly, will you?

4. Maintain maximum mental capacity.

National surveys continue to indicate that the overwhelming majority of Americans believe that our nation is headed in the wrong direction while others believe we are coming to the close of the age. Apocalyptic warnings seem to be swirling all around us amidst accelerating moral decline.

The scriptural admonition for the days in which we're living is clear: *"The end of all things is near. Therefore be alert and of sober mind so you can pray (1 Pet. 4:7, NIV).* Pot smoking fosters just the opposite.

Joseph Califano, head of the National Center on Addiction and Substance Abuse, declares without qualification that "pot smoking adversely affects motor skills and does serious damage to the brain over the long-term." Objective studies repeatedly show that regular users find their IQ dropping and all cognitive functions hindered.

A recent study from Northwestern University established clearly that teen "potheads" had brain abnormalities related to poor short-term memory performance. Healthy individuals who did not use marijuana scored thirty-seven times better on average than users—not just addicts—who had smoked pot in the past.

Morning Joe cohost Joe Scarborough said on national TV recently that he never smoked pot. "Why do I want to make my odds for success even longer? It just makes you dumb!"

The Executive Director of Drug Free America Foundation in St. Petersburg, Florida, Calvina Fay, makes an even stronger case: "It's a big lie to say marijuana is not harmful. We are fooling ourselves if we think legalizing drugs is not going to be extremely detrimental to our children." She knows it's only common sense that people of any age who are toking up are going to adversely affect their minds and alter their consciousness.

Matthew Leahy was in the newspapers a short time ago, where it stated he started smoking marijuana at fourteen, experienced a drop in grades, and then eventually ended up in a mental hospital where he hung himself. A more uplifting testimony is the one I heard personally of a ninth grader who regularly smoked pot which "really messed up my mind" but he was grateful to God that he had been set free from the addiction that was ruining his life.

This all may seem so self-evident but let's face it; many parents are reluctant to speak out against this because they feel hypocritical, having experimented when they were younger. Moms and dads, your children's lives are at stake! Sit down and share transparently that you were acting stupidly many decades ago, but now, from real experience, you know the dangers and care enough to wave the red flag: "Bridge out! Stop. Don't go there!"

5. Protect public safety.

Many marijuana advocates will tell you that we already allow alcohol, so why shouldn't we allow pot? Granted, beer and wine and adult beverages have been around for thousands of years and unfortunately some people abuse them. Scripture speaks of "moderation" here and "obeying the governing authorities" (Rom. 13:1-8) regarding laws. Adult beverages are a cultural reality and it was foolishness when people tried to "prohibit" their usage because, in fact, the Bible doesn't prohibit their responsible use.

Just because some people overindulge and do harm due to alcohol is not a valid reason to exacerbate the situation by adding dope to the mix! I'm sure you've heard the adage, "Don't point to bad behavior to justify more bad behavior."

Here's the deal:

- In 2015 the National Institute on Alcohol Abuse released a study saying that "30% of Americans admitted they struggled with alcohol in their lives."

- Thirty-three thousand Americans are killed yearly in traffic accidents—one third because of drunk drivers. How many others are left impaired or paralyzed for life?

- One-point-two million drivers are arrested annually for drunk driving. The highest number is among twenty-one to twenty-five-year-olds.

- One in three people will be involved in a drunk-driving crash in their lifetime.

- Car crashes are the leading cause of deaths for teens. Teenage alcohol use kills over 48,000 every year.

- Drunk driving costs you and me $132 billion a year.

Be honest with yourself: In light of the above, do you want to compound these sobering statistics by making marijuana freely available?

A deterrent to drinking and driving is the alcohol aroma on one's breath. That basically goes out the window when people think they can smoke a few joints outside, drive "high" down the highway and never dream of one day standing before a judge with a weeping father who lost the love of his life and three children via an intoxicated driver. Think about it along with the prison term and lifetime of guilt that follows.

By the way, the pop stars, comedians, politicians, and marijuana pushers won't be standing with you in that court room. They might be perusing their latest issue of *Rolling Stone*, discovering new ways to promote pot in between occasional, unfortunate stories on celebrities who have "bit the dust" from pursuing the hedonistic lifestyle they applaud.

6. Don't relinquish control of your life.

Our culture attempts to airbrush away sin and its consequences as it emphasizes a message: indulge yourself (instead of "control yourself"). Yet there are three maxims of life from which we cannot escape:

1. Life is a series of choices.

2. Choices bring consequences (eventually, not always immediately).

3. Choices determine destiny.

As people increasingly get "stoned" and yield the control of their lives to ingested substances that bring temporary "highs," the results are weaker individuals and a weaker nation. Über-liberal *Newsweek* editor, Tina Brown, released a statement recently in which she said, "Legal weed contributes to us being a fatter, dumber, sleepier nation even less able to compete with the Chinese."

Scripture tells us that our lives are to be surrendered to God and we are to draw upon His grace to resist temptations that can bring us into destructive enslavement to sin. Jesus cautioned us when he said, *"I tell you most solemnly that anyone who chooses a life of sin is trapped in a dead end life and is, in fact, a slave" (Jn 8:34 MSG).*

The fact is, marijuana easily becomes habit-forming in the lives of people, especially impressionable youth. It oftentimes becomes a "gateway" to other drugs.

The most successful ministry that has helped bring deliverance to thousands of drug-addicted young people is Teen Challenge, with a track record of over forty years. Jack Smith, president of the Teen Challenge USA chapter in Missouri says, "Our experience is that marijuana is a gateway drug leading to harder and more damaging drugs. Well over half our students indicate the first drug they really were involved with was marijuana."

Government agencies such as the FDA and the Drug Enforcement Administration have all published reports showing, over the years, the addictive nature of marijuana. Try it once; try it again; when things get tough, a "buzz" beats reality any day!

USA Today reported the following in an article on addiction and marijuana: "A group of addiction counselors and physicians said they're seeing more marijuana addiction problems, especially in youths, and that wider pot availability will exacerbate the problem."

"This is just throwing gas on the fire," said Ben Cort of the Colorado Center for Dependency, Addiction and Rehabilitation at the University of Colorado hospital.

Pop-culture paints a glamorous and enticing picture of a life with pot and uninhibited "freedom." Miley Cyrus lights up a joint on stage and the crowd hoots and hollers approval. Strip off clothes and get on the wrecking ball to swing naked across the room in her video viewed by over three million.

The book of Proverbs paints a different picture and it's not too flattering. Repetitious sinful activity is likened to a "dog returning to its vomit" (Prov. 26:11). This is an aphorism referring to foolish people who lack moral behavior and repeat indulgence in activities that bring about their inevitable ruin.

The pro-marijuana magazine, *High Times*, won't tell you this. Remember that cryptic line in the Eagles song, "You can check out anytime you like, but you can never leave"?

7. Be responsible and care for our children.

Jesus Christ, the most influential person who ever lived in human history, demonstrated genuine care and concern for children. Not only did He heal them but he strongly rebuked His disciples when they tried to keep them away. He warned us, *"But if anyone causes one of these little ones who believe in Me to sin, it would be better for him to have a large millstone hung around his neck and to be drowned in the depths of the sea" (Matt. 18:6).*

Now let's get real. When we talk about legalizing marijuana, what message are we sending to this next generation? "It's legal. It's okay. Like cigarettes, it's the adult thing to do. Don't worry about getting caught. Today they just wink at you anyway—give you a ticket, with no arrest and no record!"

Clever politicians rationalize and assure voters they'll have stringent regulations to keep pot out of young people's hands.

Fearful and selfish parents are caving because they don't want to alienate their child and, after all, juveniles have to experiment and find out about life for themselves.

One TV commentator went so far as to say "Let's give it a go—these are laboratories of democracy," referring to municipalities legalizing pot. In other words, why don't we just give it a try and evaluate down the road? After all we've had other social experiments like the welfare state…no-fault divorce…abortion on demand… They've been disasters and have brought devastating consequences to millions of lives (and over fifty-five million unborn) but, hey, what the heck, let's see what happens.

"Although they claimed to be wise, they became fools…" (Rom. 1:22).

On this point, we cannot and must not be silent. We cannot offer up our precious little ones and future generations on the altar of selfishness and hedonistic pleasure. To deceive ourselves by saying we will just keep it out of their hands is sheer lunacy. Think of how many parents' liquor cabinets, refrigerators, and medicine cabinets have been raided easily by youth tempted to experiment!

How about the sixteen-year-old boy who recently got a hold of some drugs and alcohol and then drove a car, killing four people and paralyzing another?

- One in six young people who try marijuana before age eighteen will either abuse it or will become addicted.—National Institutes of Health

- Teenagers using pot before age eighteen are two to four times more likely to develop psychoses as young adults, compared to those who don't.

- "We are fooling ourselves if we think legalizing drugs is not going to be extremely detrimental to our children."—Executive Director of Drug Free America Foundation, St. Petersburg, Florida

A Little Long but Long Overdue

Here's the deal: this commentary had to be comprehensive and not merely a few bullet points for easy reading. We must face up to the coming tsunami! This is a perfect storm gaining daily momentum and it must be stopped in its tracks before it is too late.

I would encourage you to watch a documentary called *Narco Culture*. It does what I'm endeavoring to do with this commentary— raise awareness of what can happen if we do not awaken to what's happening concerning the push to legalize pot and other drugs.

The focus is on Juarez, Mexico and what has happened there in a brief time as drugs became increasingly accepted and promoted. It's very personal for me since I planted churches in both Juarez and its sister city across the border in El Paso, Texas.

What was once a beautiful and peaceful Mexican city is now a drug-infested war zone. El Paso was labeled "the most peaceful city in the USA" with only five homicides a year. Juarez records over 3500 homicides in a year! Most small businesses are closed. Fear and assassinations abound with bombs, AK-47s, and decapitations. Narco-culture music is very popular with the youth who are now living amidst the legalized and illegal drug culture.

The most poignant part of the film comes at the end where a massive rally is being held in Durango. An Hispanic woman speaks passionately as she calls the people to "awaken in our city to gain awareness of what happened in Juarez and realize it can be here next! Mexico is being destroyed unless we change!"

I appeal to you, the reader, to heed this woman's warning as the United States of America hangs in the balance.

Not long ago, a 30-something woman in Las Vegas plowed her car into pedestrians walking the sidewalks. She killed one and maimed 35 others—innocent men, women, and children. This was a tragedy with roots: she was "high" on marijuana.

Chapter 30
Suicide and Death with Dignity

What Happens to People Who Take Their Own Lives?
"Is mercy killing...death with dignity...euthanasia all right?"

"What happens to people who kill themselves?"

"Do Christians automatically go to hell if they take their own life?"

"Is suicide the unpardonable sin?"

"Suicide is caused by depression, a disease, so people aren't responsible, correct?"

"Aren't sensitive subjects like this best left to medical-health professionals?"

"The term 'suicide' isn't in the Bible, so who are we to judge?"

When Robin Williams killed himself, celebrities, reporters, politicians, and even preachers tried to comfort mourners with comments like the following: "He finally found peace;" "He's up there making God and angels laugh"; "He's gone to a better place"; and, the Academy of Motion Picture Arts and Sciences tweeted a sentimental photo of Aladdin hugging Genie with the caption, "Genie, you're free!"

Williams tragically hanged himself with a belt around his neck. The Bible directs Christians to put on "the full armor of God" starting with the "belt of truth" (Eph. 6:10-13). What brought him death can symbolize life if we embrace the truth.

Personally, I believe when there is an untimely death, it's wise to withhold comments for a season to allow people time to reflect and grieve. Job's friends were silent for seven days before they spoke. Ecclesiastes 3 tells us there is a "time to weep... mourn... keep silence, and a time to speak." Premature comments may prove hurtful and do more harm than good.

We are ending our thirty-day Bullseye Challenge on this topic as questions about the afterlife abound, people try to advocate euthanasia increasingly in our culture, and agents of change involved in social justice must look out for others, especially the most vulnerable in our midst.

A Sensitive Subject—Suicide
Suicide is a choice to intentionally take one's own life. It comes from the Latin words sui ("of oneself ") and cid ("to kill").

In America there is a suicide every thirteen minutes. Thirty-eight thousand deaths yearly are attributed to suicide, and the figure is increasing. It's the leading cause of death among fifteen- to twenty-four-year-olds, and for those in their mid-forties to mid-sixties there has been a thirty percent increase in the last decade. Ironically, psychiatrists have the highest suicide rate among the medical professions.

People in the Bible who either took their lives or wanted to die include: Saul, Moses, Elijah, Jonah, Zimri, Ahithophel, Abimelech, and Judas. Samson collapsed a building on himself, but I view this as martyrdom since he is honored in Hebrews 11 for his redemptive heroics.

Here's the deal: Suicide is not God's will, and although it is not the unpardonable sin (unbelief and rejection of Christ), it is a most dangerous and very serious sin. Amidst the worst struggles of life, God always remains "an anchor for the soul, firm and secure" (Heb. 6:19).

Sadly, there are countless millions who have no relationship with God to avail themselves of His help in the time of need, although some do cry out in their anguish, and only God knows what transpires in those closing seconds. We do well to avoid speculation here.

Others suffer from genuine mental illness, debilitating depression and biological disorders that can cloud/impair their judgment so they do not think clearly and rationally in the throes of their crisis. Yes, suicide is sin, but is it at times a sin not leading to eternal death (1 John 5:17)? Again, we need to tread very carefully here.

If a person is genuinely saved as a result of repentance and faith in Jesus Christ, family and friends should hold fast to the salvation promise of John 5:24 in which a person "has ever-lasting life, and shall not come into judgment, but has passed from death to life."

> *Romans 8:38-39 states, "neither death nor life... shall be able to separate us from the love of God which is in Christ Jesus our Lord."*

On the other hand, Christians should never presume on the grace of God and risk gambling their eternal destiny by suicide. Every one of us should walk in a healthy fear of God as we reflect on warnings in Scripture:

- Hebrews 10:26-31 cautions about sinning will-fully and calls the genuineness of our salvation into question.

- Revelation 21:8 declares that murderers (suicide is a grave sin equivalent to murder) *"shall have their part in the lake of fire."*

- *"If anyone destroys the temple of God, God will destroy him. For the temple of God is holy, which temple you are" (1 Cor. 3:17).*

This divine tension in which God keeps us is a beautiful and mysterious thing. He is the Author of life who ultimately has the authority to give and take this precious gift. We affirm this and say with Job, *"I came naked from my mother's womb, and I shall have nothing when I die. The Lord gave me everything I had, and they were His to take away. Blessed be the name of the Lord!" (Job 1:21, TLB).*

Jesus revealed Satan as a *"murderer"* and the *"father of lies" (John 8:44).* It is this enemy of our soul who whispers "Life is not worth living"... "I can't go on"... "It'll only get worse"... "I'd be better off in the next life"... Yet while the *"thief comes only to steal, kill and destroy,"* it is Jesus who reminds us, *"but I have come that you might have life and have it in abundance" (John 10:10).*

Delving Into Depression

Depression is real and, like it or not, it oftentimes stems from sinful choices and consequences. Let's mention this first before citing other legitimate causes that are not necessarily sin-related. This is critical because too often commentators and counselors attribute suicide only to external causes—things that happen to us or come upon us, instead of connecting them to our own wrong choices and sinful reactions.

The cumulative effects of persistently violating God's holy standards can result in people being crushed and bitter, then blaming God for their fate. *"When a man's folly brings his way to ruin, his heart rages against the Lord" (Prov. 19:3).*

Let's be honest: as our society has drifted increasingly away from Judeo-Christian foundations, suicides have increased dramatically especially among the young and middle-aged baby boomers. How much of our pain, suffering, and sleeplessness is really sin-related?

Studies show that in Europe the suicide rate has increased dramatically as Biblical standards have been discarded over the decades. How much of this pain, restlessness, lack of peace, stress, and infirmity is connected to sinful behavior causing masses to seek medication like antidepressants (as well as alcohol, marijuana, and hard drugs) for escape and temporary relief?

Consumer Reports magazine, not long ago, did a cover story on pain and pills. The cover story says it all: "America is in Pain—and Being Killed by Painkillers." Prescription-drug use has skyrocketed 300 percent in just ten years! Sin abounds, bringing STDs, aches, stress, back problems, migraines, and joint maladies to multitudes who will not obey a loving and holy God.

Millions of people today feel depressed ("pressed down") but don't know why. Depression is not the root problem. The guilt people sense and try to dismiss is actually God convicting us and "pressing down" upon us that we might employ the privilege of confession and cleansing of conscience to find forgiveness and freedom in Him! Read Psalm 32 for the testimony of a liberated man sharing his beautiful redemptive story.

"He that keeps the law, happy is he" (Prov. 29:18).
"But the wicked are like the troubled sea, when it cannot rest, whose waters cast up mire and dirt. 'There is no peace,' says my God, 'for the wicked'" (Isa. 57:20).

Boyhood is a movie that has been extolled by critics as a "Masterpiece!" It's twelve years in a boy's life recorded in real time. The story unfolds with fornication, two divorces, debt, lying, physical and verbal abuse, drunkenness, drugs, profanity, destruction of property, exploitation of women, self-pity, out-of-wedlock birth, deceit, mockery of Christianity, thievery, dishonoring of parents, pornography, and a closing scene featuring a woman sobbing while reviewing her life and saying, "I just thought there'd be more!" The characters' lives apart from God could easily bring them to a place of suicide. Tragic.

Multitudes of deceived people need to be helped in seeing that their problem of depression is self-induced and not something that mysteriously and arbitrarily comes upon folks like measles or the flu. Our job is to reach out and help these folks with the gospel and God's truth.

A man was desperate and depressed. He went to an old buddy who counseled him to go and talk with a psychiatrist. He did but it brought no relief and neither did the meds. So the friend advised him to invest in a therapist. He did but his money was running out and the attempts at coping didn't deliver. Finally his friend told him of a circus in a nearby town where there was a clown who was hilarious and made everybody laugh. The deflated man began to cry and when he looked up he said, "I know that won't work because, you see, I am that clown."

Entertainment Weekly magazine once proclaimed Robin Williams the "Funniest Man Alive." Maybe his long-standing battle with depression was not primarily from the sin factor but from something that unfortunately many don't or won't consider.

The enigmatic, energetic Williams said after undergoing serious heart surgery that the experience left him "feeling like a mortal for the first time in my life, and I didn't like how that felt." Resorting to doing more sequels discouraged him and when his attempts at a TV show failed, it was a dark day. Plus paying off two wives was "ripping his heart out through the wallet."

The onslaught of Parkinson's disease weighed heavily as it attacks mobility and persona. Someone in his inner circle told *In Touch* magazine, "His last words were, 'I just can't take it anymore. The pain is too much.'"

The tragedy provides a look beneath any smiling veneer and projected image. *"Laughter can conceal a heavy heart, but when the laughter ends, the grief remains" (Prov. 14:13, NLT).*

Five Suicide-Related Situations

1. Intentional Suicide

    In America there is a suicide every thirteen minutes. Many of these tragedies involve people who intentionally, deliberately, and willingly take their own life.

    Suicide is not the will of God and although it is not the unpardonable sin (unbelief and rejection of Jesus Christ); it is a grave transgression against our Creator who commands us not to murder (suicide is equivalent to murder). He is the Author of life, who ever remains "an anchor for the soul, firm and secure" (Heb. 6:19).

    The eternal destiny of someone in deep depression and deception, communicating remorsefully to God in closing minutes, repenting of sins and truly putting his trust in Jesus Christ alone as his Lord and Savior (which is what the Bible teaches is essential for salvation [Rom. 10:9]), is a matter we must entrust to a just and loving God. In these most difficult situations, we must never presume on God or communicate an image of God that is not aligned with scripture.

    "My God would never send a person to hell!"

    Actually, your "God" is a product of your own imagination, inconsistent with the holy and merciful God revealed in the Bible. Hell, created for the devil and his demons, is real and it is the eternal destination for all who reject the gospel (good news), the "free gift of eternal life in Jesus Christ our Lord" (Rom. 6:23).

2. Mentally Impaired Suicide

    "I fear for the future"..."I'm afraid what's going to happen"..."I'm so stressed out and depressed. I'm fearful all the time. It's getting worse!"

    Jesus described the end of the age with *"men's hearts failing them for fear, and for looking after those things which are coming on the earth..." (Lk 21:26).*

Those of us who are spiritually, emotionally, and mentally healthy easily declare, *"There is no fear in love; but perfect love casts out fear: because fear has torment."* *(1 Jn 4:18)*. We add: *"God hasn't given us a spirit of fear but of love, power and a sound mind"* *(2 Tim. 1:7)*.

What if someone does not have that "sound mind"? What should we do when we encounter situations where someone committed suicide after battling tormenting fears, debilitating depression, biological disorders and forms of mental illness that clouded their judgment so they weren't thinking clearly and rationally in the throes of their crisis?

- Military veterans with Post Traumatic Stress Disorder

- Women with severe postpartum or menopausal depression

- Fragile individuals experiencing multiple surgeries and "cocktail" meds resulting in chemical imbalances, confusion, and dark depression

- Godly people like Rick Warren's twenty-seven-year-old son, Matthew, who was rescued many times from the brink of suicide but killed himself after a lifelong battle with mental illness. Rick put it this way: "My son took his life. It was his choice. He was a young man with a tender heart and a tortured mind."

What does God mean when he instructs us to *"comfort the feebleminded, support the weak, be patient towards all men"* *(1 Thess. 5:14)?*

We must be careful not to oversimplify or spiritualize. "Just pray it away!"… "Cast that thing out!"…"Confess the Word!"…"Man up, wimp!"…"Go put your big girl pants on, girl!"

Don't hear what I'm not saying here. God does tell us to renew our minds, confess His Word, lay hold of His promises, and persevere amidst life's adversities. Yet sometimes folks face such overwhelming and life–threatening hardships that they declare with Paul and his team, *"We were under great pressure, far beyond our ability to endure, so that we despaired even of life. Indeed, in our hearts we felt the sentence of death" (2 Cor. 1:8-9).*

Paul did go on to state, *"But this happened that we might not rely on ourselves but on God, who raises the dead. He has delivered us from such a deadly peril, and he will deliver us. On Him we have set our hope that he will continue to deliver us..." (2 Cor. 9b-10).*

The challenge is moving from point A to point B without succumbing to hopelessness. A key ingredient is what Paul stated, "as you will help us by your prayers" (v. 11), and compassionate support.

A long time colleague of mine, Jim, gives out his personal testimony tract entitled, "Snatched From the Brink of Suicide!"

Sheila Walsh, an internationally known singer at Billy Graham Crusades and former co-host of the *700 Club*, says, "In the morning I was seen across the nation on TV and that night I was locked in a ward of a psychiatric hospital at the age of 34." She honestly believed that her life was over and things were hopeless as she spiraled into darkness and a nervous breakdown.

But like Jimmy Stewart's character in *It's a Wonderful Life*, God brought her back from the brink and today she's the author of *Life is Tough, But God is Faithful*, speaking at conferences and ministering hope to multitudes who may be right on life's edge.

Famous Christian leaders like Charles Spurgeon, David Brainard, J. B. Phillips, Abraham Lincoln, and C.S. Lewis all battled depression. When Mr. Lewis's beloved wife died he wrote "A Grief Observed" under a pseudonym lest anybody discover his near despair.

In these perilous times, may we nurture a culture of transparency so no one has to hide the struggles within. And as caring Christians, may we be ambassadors of hope and understanding in these sensitive areas.

3. Accidental Suicide

Ever hear of the movie *Sin City*? It's based on extremely dark graphic novels featuring people being slaughtered sadistically. Their slogan is "Sin City. Come for the fun—stay for your funeral." This is the sad reality for scores of pleasure-seekers today.

Last summer I spoke with a young man in his mid-twenties who is married with a little daughter. After I inquired how he met his mate, he told me that both of them were committed into a psych ward after each had attempted suicide. Between the two of them there were five divorces among parents and sinful patterns that brought them to the point of despair. God miraculously saved them and after they were married they embraced the call of God on their lives for ministry to reach young people.

What about multitudes, especially young people, who are seduced by the allure of our culture and before they hear the gospel (or having responded previously are drifting) spiral off into drugs, alcohol, recklessness, and deviant sexual practices that destroy lives? Burdened by guilt, shame, and the inevitable consequences of sin, they attempt suicide to escape.

This is a delicate one. As a child had they experienced a genuine conversion and now were in a wayward state? (Don't dismiss childhood conversions as our son, who is currently pastoring in Georgia, genuinely came to Christ when he was three!)

With drug experimentation, did things go awry and an overdose occurred that was not really a suicide at all?

Was a son, daughter, or spouse attempting to get the attention of loved ones and their threat became a tragic, accidental reality? I thank God that He spared a dear friend at whose marriage I officiated years after she had been rescued by God after ingesting sixty-four Advils in a moment of foolish desperation.

Was it a prank that backfired? A father once told me that his son viewed *Schindler's List* and later decided to scare his brother by reenacting a hanging. Tragically his

brother found him hanging by the noose, which suffo-
cated him.

Because of pornography and rampant perversion in
our culture, some people are found in suicidal hangings
or at least that's what observers initially conclude. Actually they've engaged in erotic asphyxiation that backfired. You may recall David Carradine, the actor who
was found hanging in the closet in an apparent suicide
that was later ruled "accidental erotic asphyxiation."

In situations like these, one should be very tender-
hearted and careful with what is communicated. While
we don't want to give false assurance, we mustn't alienate
grieving friends and relatives either. I usually state something like this: "In this painful time of grieving, let's reflect on the positives in his/her life. We can trust God who
is all-loving and just. What is critical now is what we can
individually learn from the situation, plus make sure our
relationship is right with the living God. If the deceased
could return, that would be their top concern, I'm sure."

4. Avoidance Suicide
   Important Preface:

Approaching this area, let me state up front that I am
not advocating anything, but simply addressing something that happens and shouldn't be avoided in this topic. Consider an example.

Some who have concussions and find themselves
in highly stressful situations may not respond ideally.
They can exhibit dramatic mood swings, confusion, and
sleep deprivation, and act out of character.

"Pressure reveals the person," but if the person is in
a weakened state they may choose avoidance at a critical time. My appeal is that we don't heartlessly condemn people to eternal damnation when God calls us to
be understanding.

After the Bible, one of the classics that has pro-
foundly influenced Christians for centuries is *Fox's
Book of Martyrs*. Reading the accounts of believers

undergoing unbelievable persecution and yet shining as beacon lights inspires leaders in every generation.

Knowing *"Dying grace does not come until the dying hour"* and that *"God's grace is sufficient for us and His power is made perfect in weakness" (2 Cor. 12:9)*, this fourth situation requires acute sensitivity to the Holy Spirit. May we never have to face the persecution others do in the world, but it's important we be prepared even as we believe God can supernaturally rescue anyone in any circumstance at any time.

If someone faces extreme, brutal savagery leading to an inevitable, torturous death, might God in His all-encompassing mercy make allowance for somebody bringing his life to an end? For those who believe that suicide is always murder warranting eternal damnation, please consider the following.

Last week in Virginia I had a meeting with a long-standing Christian leader. He related to me the unbelievable persecution Christians face in North Korea. I will be discreet but he described imprisoned Christians brought out into the open and raped, giving birth and having their newborns thrown to the dogs before their eyes.

The publication "Voice of the Martyrs" has communicated scenes like the following: Christians are martyred in one nation by being made to lie down on the pavement and slowly and systematically having their feet then legs then torso crushed by heavy vehicles in hard-to-imagine, agonizing killings.

With ISIS in Iraq where individuals are openly beheaded, women and children are hacked to death and men face unfathomable, torturous deaths if they will not convert to Islam, do you think God extends mercy to some who fall on a sword, drink poison, or flee knowing they will be immediately gunned down?

If someone is overwhelmed by terror dreading a savage, inevitable death and cries out to God in repentance for ending their life, do you really believe God would sentence them to hell? Can the God who forgave Moses, David, and Paul for their participation in murder extend mercy in these types of extenuating and excruciating circumstances?

Islamic suicide-bombers who believe in jihad believe they have automatic assurance of heaven and seventy-two virgins for their suicide. This is deception.

I, for one, don't believe it's deception to believe that persecuted and incapacitated Christians in certain circumstances can be reprieved for hastening inevitable death to be ushered into the presence of the living God. Feel free to respectfully disagree.

5. Physician-Assisted Suicide/"Death with Dignity"

In 1976 I got married. That same year I also had a book in my possession by Dr. Francis Schaeffer entitled *How Should We Then Live?* The title comes from Ezekiel 33:10, which is an urgent prophetic warning for America today.

The book changed my life. For over forty-three years in full-time vocational ministry I have lived its message. The frightening part is that the warning given by Francis Schaeffer is unfolding before our eyes yet more people know about the marriage of Brad Pitt and Angelina Jolie than this reality.

Here's the deal: As we remove God and His commands from our culture and fail to uphold the sanctity of life (everyone is created in the image of God), we are on a slippery slope to our demise. Our only hope is for a genuine spiritual awakening and that is something I give my life for each and every day.

Euthanasia comes from the Greek words meaning "good death." Alternative and equally misleading terms used for actively taking someone's life are "mercy killing," "death with dignity," and "physician-assisted suicide."

Scripture tells us that all life is sacred and the command is clear: "You shall not murder" (Ex. 20:13). The seriousness of this is seen when David ordered capital punishment for the man who assisted Saul in his suicide act (2 Sam.1:1-16). Yet euthanasia proponents like Dr. Phillip Nitchkie say, "Many people I meet and argue with believe that human life is sacred. I do not..."

The further our Western civilization drifts from our Judeo-Christian foundations, the more countries embrace euthanasia coupled with abortion and infanticide. Euthanasia is now legal in Belgium, Columbia, India, Ireland, Luxembourg, Mexico, and the Netherlands (with the Netherlands's small population they still euthanize 2000 people yearly, plus now have guidelines for infant euthanasia). Seventy-three percent of French doctors admit using drugs to end an infant's life.

This is gaining ground in America as we now see physician-assisted suicide legal in Washington, Oregon, Montana, Vermont, and New Mexico. Barring revival, it is coming to a neighborhood near you!

With economic debt skyrocketing, the baby-boomer population aging (seventy-eight million strong) and socialized medicine becoming more and more a reality, we need to make preparation now for end-of-life decisions as "death panels" will slowly be introduced as they are in Canada and elsewhere.

When my wife and I worked on our "Living Will" (P.S.: You need one and should address it now lest you lose savings and possessions in probate court plus others will make dying decisions for you!) we incorporated, end-of-life guidelines that can be obtained from "The National Right to Life."

The smooth and seductive reasoning presented by advocates of euthanasia needs to be exposed and resisted vigorously by people of faith. Doctors helping "suffering" elderly people or those with dementia, depression, or severe injuries being "put out of their misery" with lethal doses of medicine is contrary to the will of God.

Now there is a clear difference between actively killing someone and passively allowing a person to yield to inevitable death as we see in the Bible with Jesus, Stephen, Jacob, and others. This is not suicide. Also, our Christian faith requires us to compassionately care for all people approaching death as well as those with reasonable hope of recovery. Even King David nearing death was granted a young, beautiful virgin to lie in bed next to him and keep him warm (with no romantic intimacy)!

When it is obvious to all that death is at hand; there is no reasonable hope of recovery; extraordinary life support measures aren't advisable; and, the dying individual desires (ideally with family) to be allowed to "walk through the valley of the shadow of death," then the appointed time has arrived to meet one's Maker!

Consider Billy Graham's wife, Ruth, and how she concluded her days on earth. Valiantly battling persistent infirmities plus struggling with pneumonia and being bedridden, "At her request and in concert with her family, she stopped receiving nutrients through a feeding tube for her last few days hastening her death."

Sometimes an individual refuses chemotherapy when told they are in stage four terminal cancer. While not refusing minimal nourishment, others refuse a feeding tube and other extraordinary measures so as not to delay but hasten their home-going experience.

My seventy-four-year-old father attended a Sunday morning church service and then came home, sat in a chair, and begin to read a devotional book when he lowered his head and passed into the presence of the Lord.

My eighty-seven-year-old mother was flanked by my sister and me as we swabbed her lips, gently encouraged her to let go, and as I read the ninety-first Psalm she yielded her spirit as I said these words, *"For He will command his angels concerning you to guard you in all your ways; they will lift you up in their hands..."*

"She's gone!" exclaimed my sister.

"Precious in the sight of the Lord is the death of his saints" (Ps.116:15).

Epilogue
Commission

One of baseball's greatest hitters of all time died not long ago at the age of fifty-four. Hall of Famer Tony Gwynn hit over .300 for nineteen consecutive seasons, something only the legendary Ty Cobb accomplished.

Before passing away, he recorded a video message appealing for baseball players not to follow his example with smokeless tobacco, which most certainly was the cause of his death from mouth cancer. This is the same thing that the famous "Marlboro Man" did to assuage his guilt before he died prematurely from the cigarettes he advertised.

Dying declarations can have a profound effect. It's the time when people are most honest and what they say matters the most.

When the time comes for your grand finale, have you ever pondered what you would want to say? While claiming the promise of Psalm 91:16, "With long life will I satisfy him...," there is merit to reflecting on this once-in-a-lifetime opportunity. Knowing that dying grace doesn't come until the dying hour, don't project yourself into the circumstances but do give some thought to what you'd want to say. I'd like to offer a suggestion before our commission.

Departing Declarations of Those Who Didn't Live Lives for Christ
Let's pause at this juncture and examine some of the sad statements left by those who apparently led lives apart from the loving Lordship of Jesus Christ. These people speak to us from beyond the grave to

live wisely and not foolishly. Remember, *"Only one life, t'will soon be passed. Only what's done for Christ will last."*

- Music legend Kurt Cobain of Nirvana blew his brains out with a shotgun after writing that he was a "miserable, self-destructive, death-rocker...hateful towards all humans in general."

- Freddie Mercury was the flamboyant front man for supergroup, Queen (a term for a male homosexual). The gay glam rocker was said to have the greatest pure voice in rock-n-roll history. His life of narcotics and debauchery caused Elton John to declare, "He could-out party me!" He died of AIDS and was in excruciating pain when even clothing touched his skin. His parting statement is best captured by the title of his final video, *These Are the Days of Our Lives*. Makes you want to weep.

- Actress Joan Crawford rebuked her housekeeper who began praying as Joan was dying: "Damn it... don't you dare ask God to help me!"

- Lecherous Henry VIII pleaded for spiritual support in beseeching, "All is lost! Monks! Monks! Monks!"

- Author of the dark side, Edgar Allan Poe, cried, "Lord, help my poor soul!"

- Occultist Aleister Crowley shrieked, "I am perplexed! Satan get out!"

- Pop megastar Michael Jackson desperately pleaded for relief from the drug Propofol, on which he fatally overdosed, "More milk!"

- Archenemy of Christianity, Voltaire, when begged by a priest to renounce Satan, declined, saying, "This is no time for making enemies!"

- Frank Sinatra, who "Did it My Way" with his serial affairs, lavish escapades, and four wives, succumbed sorrowfully, uttering, "I'm losing," then breathing his last.

- Elizabeth I, Queen of England, proclaimed before dying, "All my possessions for a moment of time."

One more?

- Comedian W.C. Fields, when asked why he was reading the Bible on his deathbed commented, "I'm looking for loopholes!"

Contrast the above final statements with Christians like George Washington saying, "I am not afraid to go" or scientist Michael Faraday declaring, "I shall be with Christ, and that is enough." Some difference, huh?

Now it's your turn.

Can These Five Final Words Be Your Deathbed Declaration?
Over thirty years ago, a Christian leader who was very influential in my life spoke on a college campus and was asked this question in closing out his evening session, "Sir, if you had one message to leave with us before you depart, what would it be?"

Shortly thereafter, this nationally known leader was killed in a tragic car accident. Three decades later the response he gave the collegians still reverberates in my heart. It's a great sayonara statement worthy of emulating.

> *"If I had just one sentence to deposit in your hearts as I exit tonight it would be...My life is my message!"*

Billy Graham once was asked what he wants on his tombstone. He replied, *"He was faithful. He walked in integrity."*

The similarity is striking. Both men committed to practice what they preach. Authenticity is the core. Shouldn't it be the magnificent obsession of every true disciple of our Lord Jesus Christ?

One day as we lay on our bed ready to pass "through the valley of the shadow of death," may those gathered around us affirm that our words were authenticated by our witness.

> *"The years of a man's life are threescore and ten, or by reason of strength fourscore"* (Ps. 90:10).

Moses penned those words thousands of years ago and they remain oh, so true. He went on to say, *"So teach us to number our days, that we may apply our hearts unto wisdom" (v. 12).*

God equates wisdom with the stewardship of our days on earth. Are you wisely investing your time for His glory? Are you living a sincere (literally a "sun-tested") life that draws people to Him because observers know you're the real deal? Do you pass your days with eternity in mind, ever conscious of life's brevity?

> *"The shoes you tie in the morning can be untied by an undertaker in the evening."*

I'm not being morbid but simply challenging all of us to identify with the words of the departed leader speaking through the corridors of time, "My life is my message."

Is yours? And if you are falling short, will you make any necessary course corrections to align with authenticity?

There are two Sauls in the Bible. One's exit statement was a pathetic, *"I have played the fool and have erred exceedingly" (1 Sam. 26:21).* The other's was a triumphant, *"The time of my departure is at hand. I have fought a good fight, I have finished my course, I have kept the faith: henceforth there is laid up for me a crown of righteousness, which the Lord, the righteous judge, shall give me at that day; and not to me only, but unto all them also that love His appearing" (2 Tim. 4:6-8).*

Which Saul reflects your life and the legacy you'll leave? Determine today that "when your time comes," your life will have truly validated the gospel message we're privileged to proclaim. I commission you in your high calling as an ambassador for Jesus Christ to "hit the mark" with your life. God bless you richly as you go forth!

About the Author

Larry Tomczak is a best-selling author of ten books, including a quarter-million bestseller, with forty-three years of trusted ministry experience. He is a cultural commentator whose weekly articles appear on sites reaching twenty-six million monthly. He is a public policy advisor with Liberty Counsel legal defense organization and forty-year board member of Intercessors for America national prayer ministry.

He has ministered internationally and spoken to numerous NFL and NBA teams. Married for forty years, Larry and Doris have four grown children and five grandchildren.

Larry Tomczak served as student body president at Cleveland State University before working at the AFL-CIO headquarters across from the White House in Washington, DC. He then entered full-time ministry and has served in this vocation for over forty-three years. Larry has trained leaders, established dozens of churches in America and abroad and today serves as a cultural commentator bringing insight, analysis and perspective from a Biblical worldview.

Larry has a conviction: as "David served the purpose of God in his generation and then fell asleep" (Book of Acts 13:36), if you would do the best with your life, find out what God is doing in your generation and fling yourself into it! For decades his ministry has helped individuals find and fulfill their destiny in life.

With the BULLSEYE initiative, Larry is issuing a challenge to people of all ages to become informed influencers in today's changing culture. Investing fifteen minutes for thirty days, individuals can hit the mark by understanding and communicating confidently on the controversial issues of our day. This innovative approach consists of three steps: review a video for three minutes; read an article for ten minutes; then, reflect and pray for two minutes.

In a compelling and enjoyable manner, Larry addresses these hot button issues: social justice, same-sex marriage, racial inequality, Islam, legalizing marijuana, transgenderism, atheism, living together, the apocalypse, divorce, capital punishment, abortion, affairs, immigration, AIDS and STDs, suicide, masturbation, gay Christians, sexting, death with dignity and more. His passion is for everyone to know the truth and then confidently communicate it with charity and clarity.

In a national survey, sixty-seven percent of conservative Christians said they want their church to provide them with more information—more Biblical teachings—about the issues that are so important in an election. Additionally, Barna Research revealed that ninty percent of Christian leaders believe the Bible addresses most of today's controversial issues, yet only 10 percnt said they were willing to address them! Here is a resource to supply adults and youth and pastors and everyone with what they need to be equipped and engaged in making a difference today.

Larry Tomczak has given us a gift as well as a secret weapon to become confident communicators and change agents in today's confusing world. He's calling everyone concerned about our future to take the the thirty day Bullseye challenge to change our lives and our nation.

Congratulations! You are about to begin this exciting initiative to change your life. For the next 30 days, you will invest 15 minutes each day so you will "hit the mark"—understanding and communicating truth to our topsy-turvy world. Go to www.bullseyechallenge.com to watch the videos corresponding to the chapters. Together, we will make a difference for Jesus Christ.

41053203R00143

Made in the USA
Middletown, DE
03 March 2017